Science
Olympiad

Class 08

A must have book for all
Olympiads & Talent Search Exams...

by
Bhawna Joshi

BLoOM CAP
Bloom Cap Edu Ventures Pvt. Ltd.

Bloom Cap Edu Ventures Pvt. Ltd.

✿ **Administrative & Production Office**

'Ramchhaya' 4577/15, Agarwal Road, Darya Ganj, New Delhi -110002
Tele: 011- 47630600, 43518550

✿ **ISBN :** 978-93-25519-37-4

✿ **PRICE :** ₹100.00

✿ **PO No :** TXT-XX-XXXXXXX-X-XX

For further information about the books log on to
www.bloomcap.org

Follow us on   

Preface

"Future belongs to those Who prepares for it today"

School Olympiads are National & International level competitions conducted by different Government, Non-Government & Educational Organisations with the purpose of making the children ready to face competitive exams.

The challenging Questions asked in Olympiads motivate them to learn more & more and bring out the best result with improved academic performance. The Awards & Scholarship offered by Olympiads motivate children to aspire & strive for doing better and emerge out to be the best.

Science Olympiads

Being a Scientist or Engineer or Doctor has always been a dream of each school going child. A good command over Science is a must for any of these. Questions of Science Olympiads are structured to help students to develop scientific temperament & motivate them to understand the concepts of science. They also focuses on improving existing knowledge of a student by adding more information.

'Bloom Science Olympiad Study Book Class 8' is a perfect resource to Study & Practice for Olympiad Exams and other National & State Level Talent Search Exams & Other Competitions.

Some Special Features of Bloom Science Olympiad Study Books are;

- Chapterwise Exercises having different types of Objective Questions; Analytical, Applications, Remembering etc, at par with the Olympiad Level.
- Detailed Explanation for each question.
- Olympiad Pattern Practice Sets at the end.

This book is prepared by Expert Panel with the utmost care, still if you have any suggestions regarding its improvement then feel free to contact us at olympiads@bloomcap.org. We will try to inculcate your suggestions in the further editions.

Contents

Chapter 01

Crop Production and Management

1 Mark Questions

1. Which of the following is not a cereal crop?
   (a) Maize   (b) Ragi
   (c) Bean   (d) Barley

2. Farmers often add chemical fertilisers in soil to increase their crop output. However, this practice increase the .... level in soil. Fill the blank by selecting a correct option.
   (a) acid   (b) alkaline
   (c) salt   (d) neutral

3. In a town, where water scarcity is a major issue, farmers will be advised to use which method for watering their crops?
   (a) Sprinkler   (b) Drip system
   (c) Moat   (d) Dhekli

4. Complete the analogy shown below
   Seed drill : Sowing : ..... : Removing weeds
   (a) Plough
   (b) Cultivator
   (c) Hoe
   (d) None of the above

5. Before sowing the seeds in a field, the soil is broken down to the size of grain for a better yield of crops.
   Which of the following pairs of tools can be associated with these processes?
   (a) Plough, hoe and cultivator
   (b) Tractor, hoe and seed drill
   (c) Plough, seed drill and tractor
   (d) Bullock, tiller and tractor

6. Microorganisms are known to cause various diseases in crop plants affecting the overall yield. Identify the organisms which cause disease 'blight of potato.'
   (a) Fungus   (b) Virus
   (c) Protozoan   (d) Bacteria

7. Rice and soybean are crops grown during the onset of monsoon season because
   (a) they require more water for growth
   (b) they require more sunlight
   (c) they require less temperature
   (d) All of the above

8. In three agricultural fields *P*, *Q* and *R*, crops are planted in patterns as shown below

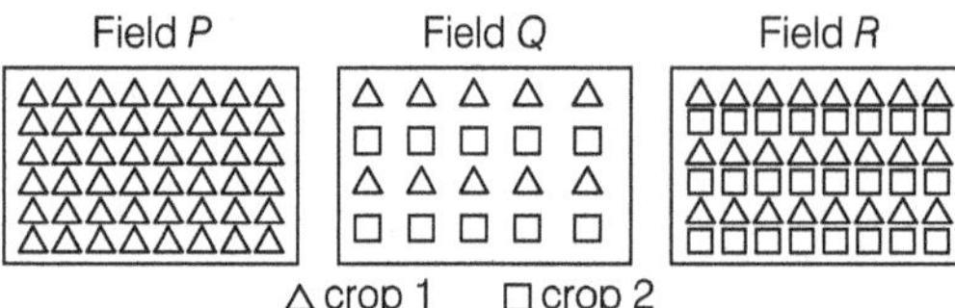

In which of the following fields, crops will grow healthy and have maximum yield?
(a) *P*
(b) *Q*
(c) *R*
(d) *P* and *R*

9. Continuous cultivation of agricultural field results in depletion of soil nutrients. Given below are some methods to restore the fertility of soil
I. Land is left uncultivated for one or more season.
II. Addition of manure to soil.
III. Excessive use of fertilisers in agricultural field.
IV. Growing different crops alternately.

Select the correct method to restore soil fertility.
Codes
(a) I and II
(b) I, II and IV
(c) III and IV
(d) All of these

10. Read the statements given below.
I. Fertilisers are used to increase the soil fertility.
II. Urea, ammonium sulphate and superphosphate are some fertilisers.

Select the option, which is correct for above statements?
(a) Both I and II are correct
(b) Only I is correct
(c) Both I and II are incorrect
(d) Only II is correct

11. Some insects or animals are listed below in the box.

> Ladybug, Locusts, Praying mantis, Ground beetle, Frog, Earthworms, Wild boar.

How many of the following can be considered as farmer's friend?
(a) 3
(b) 5
(c) 4
(d) 6

12. Identify the statement which is incorrect w.r.t the figure shown below.

(a) It is a modern method of irrigation called the sprinkler system
(b) The water available in wells, canals and lakes is lifted up using this method
(c) Its cheaper but less efficient
(d) Human labour is used in this methods

13. Study the flow chart given below.

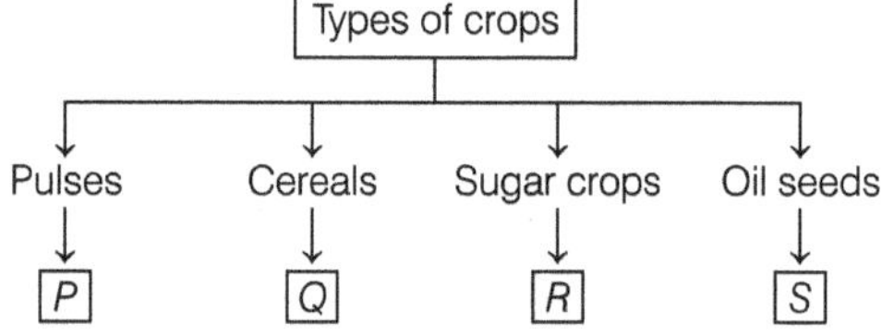

Select the correct statements w.r.t labelled parts.
(a) *P* could be ragi, while *R* could be beetroots
(b) *Q* could be beans, while *S* could be barley
(c) *P* could be legumes like gram or pea, while *S* could be mustard or groundnut
(d) *Q* could be potato or tapioca, while *R* could be sugarcane or beetroot.

2 Marks Questions

14. Match the Column I with Column II and select the correct option from codes given below.

	Column I		Column II
A.	Threshing	1.	Seed drill
B.	*Rhizobium*	2.	Separation of grain from the rest of the plant
C.	Jute	3.	Nitrogen fixation
D.	Rubber	4.	Plantation crop
E.	Broadcasting of seeds	5.	Fibre crop

Codes

	A	B	C	D	E
(a)	1	2	3	5	4
(b)	3	4	1	2	5
(c)	2	3	5	4	1
(d)	5	1	2	3	1

15. Sprinklers help in water conservation along with an efficient system of irrigation for agricultural fields.

Identify the statements which supports the above claim.

I. Sprinklers use the low pressure of water flow to irrigate the field similar to rain fall.

II. They can cover a large circular area while irrigating the fields.

III. Water drops falls directly near the roots.

IV. It prevents water logging conditions in field.

Codes

(a) I and II   (b) II and IV

(c) I, III and IV   (d) All of these

16. Refer to the figures X and Y which represent specific agricultural processes shown below.

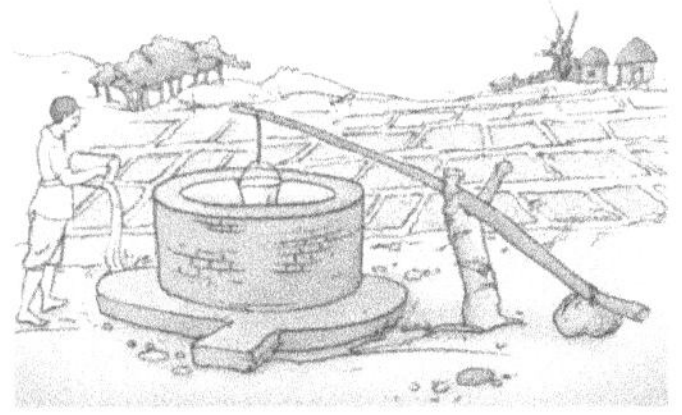

Select the correct statement w.r.t processes shown in figures X and Y.

I. X helps in removing weeds from crop plants, while Y is addition of manures to the collected crops.

II. X separates harvested grains from their stalks and Y separate grains from the chaff.

III. X is tilling, while Y is manual sowing of seeds.

Which of the following options are correct for the figure?

(a) I is correct but II and III are incorrect

(b) I and II are correct, but III is incorrect

(c) I is incorrect, but II and III are correct

(d) I and III are incorrect, but II is correct

17. Certain crops like beans, grams and peas are grown in soil where nitrogen levels need to be replenished. The main reason for adopting this practice is

I. They have *Rhizobium*, a bacteria living symbiotically within their roots.

II. These are leguminous plants.

III. They can directly absorb the atmospheric nitrogen for replenshing depleted nitrogen levels.

IV. These are non-green plants which can trap insects to absorb nitrogen.

Select the correct option.

(a) I and II   (b) I, III and IV

(c) III and IV   (d) I, II and III

Microorganisms : Friend & Foe

1 Mark Questions

1. Given below is a list of microorganisms based on their characteristic features. Pick the odd one out.
   (a) *Amoeba*   (b) *Paramecium*
   (c) *Rhizobium*   (d) *Plasmodium*

2. Which list of characteristics describe a bacterium?

	Outer layer	Cytoplasm	Nuclear material
(a)	Cell wall	Present	Circular DNA
(b)	Cell wall	Present	One or many nuclei
(c)	No cell wall	Absent	Many chromosomes
(d)	Protein coat	Absent	DNA combined with protein

3. Which of the two microorganisms live in symbiotic association in lichens?

   A. Fungus   B. Protozoa
   C. Bacteria   D. Algae

   Choose the correct option.
   (a) A and B   (b) B and C
   (c) C and D   (d) A and D

4. Observe the figures given below and identify the option which correctly pairs the organism which is chlorophyllous in nature with its figure.

   Bread mould, *Amoeba, Aspergillus, Penicillium, Chlamydomonas.*

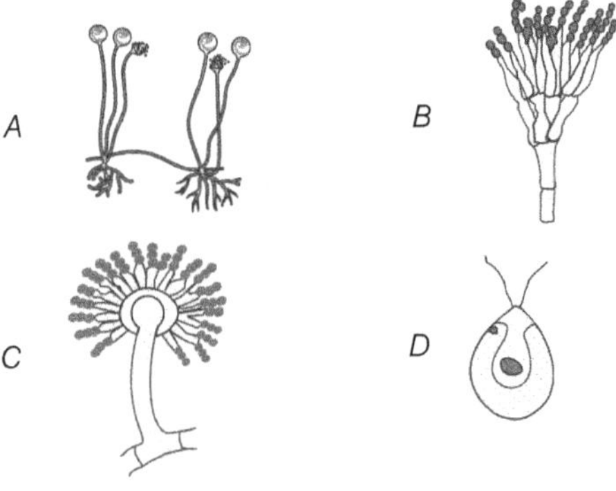

   Mark the correct option.
   (a) A - *Penicillium*
   (b) B - *Amoeba*
   (c) C - Bread mould
   (d) D - *Chlamydomonas*

5. Which of the following statements correctly corresponds to *Entamoeba?*
   I. It is a single-celled microorganism.
   II. It is classified as a plant.

III. It is classified as an animal.

IV. It is found in lakes, pond and rivers.

V. It is found as internal parasite or commensals.

Choose the correct option.

(a) I and II   (b) I and III

(c) I, IV and V   (d) II and IV

6. *X* in the figure can be identified as a fungal microorganism based on which of the following characteristics?

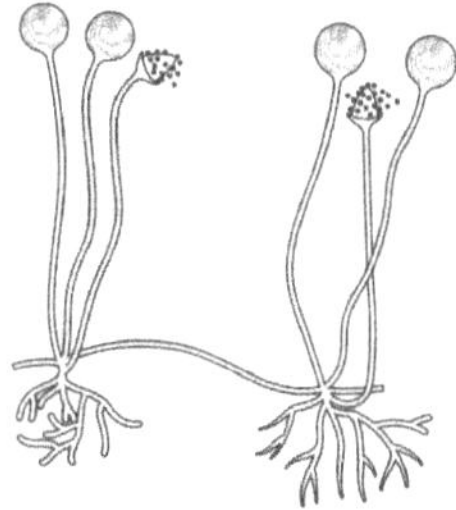

I. It is saprophyte organisms which reproduces through spores.

II. It is parasitic organisms which reproduces using host's body.

(a) Statement II is correct

(b) Both statements I and II are correct

(c) Statement I is correct

(d) None of the above

7. Bacteria have been grouped into four different types based on their shapes. Identify the different types and select the correct statements regarding them.

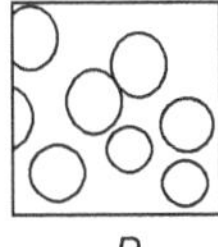
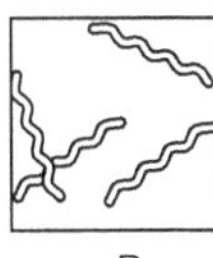
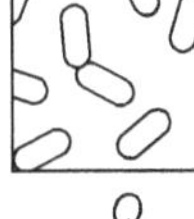
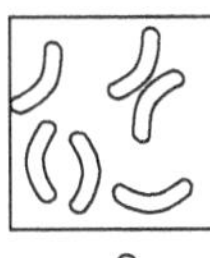

(a) *S* could be *Vibrio cholerae* which causes cholera in humans

(b) *Lactobacillus* could be an example of *P*, which helps in curdling of milk

(c) Type *R* bacteria are rod-shaped and called as bacilli.

(d) Type *Q* bacteria are comma- shaped and are called as cocci bacteria

8. Read the following statements about bacteria.

I. Bacteria are the unicellular organisms.

II. They have cell walls with defined nucleus.

III. They reproduce by binary fission and can grow very rapidly in favourable conditions.

IV. They can also reproduce sexually by exchanging genetic information through DNA or RNA.

Which of the above statement(s) is/are incorrect?

(a) I and IV   (b) Only II

(c) II and IV   (d) Only IV

9. Algae are used as food, as they are rich in carbohydrates, vitamins and few other inorganic substances. Which of the following can be considered an example of such a food?

(a) *Gelidium*

(b) *Spirogyra*

(c) *Rhodymenia*

(d) None of the above

10. In which of the following groups only bacterial diseases are paired?

(a) Rabies, small pox, AIDS and malaria

(b) Anthrax, typhoid, hepatitis and cholera

(c) Typhoid, anthrax, tuberculosis and cholera

(d) Syphilis, AIDS, rabies and influenza

11. Categorise the organisms given below as either friend or foe of humans. How many of them can be identified as beneficial for humans?

1. *Nostoc*
2. *Entamoeba*
3. *Lactobacillus*
4. *Anabaena*
5. *Aspergillus*
6. *Bacillus anthracis*
7. *Rhizobium*

(a) 4   (b) 5   (c) 6   (d) 3

12. A chemical X secreted by a bacteria/fungi can be labelled as an antibiotic when it can/is

(a) causes a disease in an individual
(b) kills or prevents the growth of bacteria in body
(c) produced as a result of a microorganism entering the body
(d) a protein made by WBCs which destroy microbes

13. Consider the statements given below.

I. Bread mould is a fungi.
II. Foot and mouth disease of cattle is caused by algae.
III. The bacterium which promotes the formation of curd is *Rhizobium*.
IV. The cyanobacteria commonly used as fertiliser is *Nostoc*.

Which of the above statements are incorrect?

(a) I and IV
(b) II and III
(c) I, II and IV
(d) I, II, III and IV

14. State (T) for True and (F) for False.

I. Protozoans feed on fungi and bacteria which are harmful to human beings.
II. Fungi are used in agriculture to enhance the fertility of soil.

III. Yeast produces CH_4 when it multiplies rapidly causing dough to rise.
IV. Citrus canker is a fungal disease transmitted through seeds.
V. Agar-agar is used in preparation of ice creams.

Codes

	I	II	III	IV	V
(a)	T	F	F	T	T
(b)	T	T	T	T	T
(c)	T	T	F	F	T
(d)	T	F	F	F	T

15. Observe and identify the process shown by the equation

$$\text{Nitrogen} \xrightarrow{\text{Bacteria}} \text{Nitrates}$$

(a) Nitrification
(b) Nitrogen-fixation
(c) Decomposition
(d) Denitrification

16. Among the organisms mentioned below, which one is capable of fixing nitrogen while living symbiotically with the roots of leguminous plants

(a) *Rhizobium*
(b) *Pseudomonas*
(c) *Clostridium*
(d) *Nostoc*

17. The nitrogen gas of the atmosphere is converted into compounds of nitrogen to be used by the plants. Which of the following helps in the process?

A. By nitrogen-fixing bacteria in soil.
B. By earthworm.
C. By lightning.
D. By *Rhizobium* in root nodules.
E. By other microorganisms such as fungi.

Choose the correct option.

(a) A and B
(b) B and C
(c) A, C, D and E
(d) B and E

2 Marks Questions

18. Milk, if left out of the refrigerator will go sour and appear as shown below in the figure. Which of the following are incorrect regarding this?

A. Viruses cause milk to go sour faster.
B. As milk goes sour, it becomes more acidic.
C. The higher the temperature, the faster the milk will go sour.
D. Bacterial action causes the milk to go sour.
E. Milk is converted into acetic acid.

Choose the option which indicates incorrect statements.

(a) A and B   (b) B and D
(c) A and E   (d) C and D

19. Given below is a list of general preventive measures.
Categorise them so as to given to the family of a patient who had been suffering from.

A. TB   B. Cholera   C. Malaria

Preventive measures

I. Spray insecticides in homes.
II. Eat properly cooked food.
III. Patient should be kept in complete isolation.
IV. Maintain personal hygiene.
V. Drink clean and boiled drinking water.
VI. Put fine wire mesh on doors and windows.

Select the appropriate option.

	A	B	C
(a)	II, I	III, IV	V, VI
(b)	III	II, IV, V	I, VI
(c)	I, VI	III, V	II, VI
(d)	I, II	III, IV	V, VI

20. The figure given below shows the nitrogen cycle.

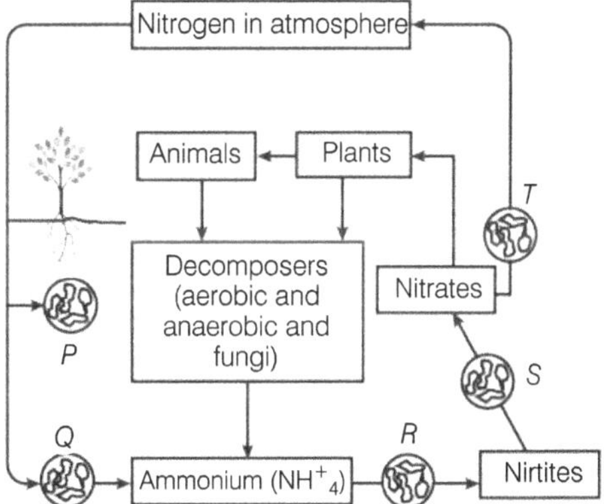

Identify the events taking place at P-T and select the correct option.

I. $P \rightarrow$ Symbiotic association of *Azospirillum*
II. $Q \rightarrow$ Ammonification of atmospheric N_2
III. R and $S \rightarrow$ Nitrification i.e., $NH_4^+ \longrightarrow NO_3^-$
IV. $T \rightarrow$ Denitrification, i.e. $NO_3^- \xrightarrow{\textit{Pseudomonas}} NO_2^-$

Codes
(a) II, III and IV
(b) III and IV
(c) I, II and IV
(d) All of these are correct

Synthetic Fibres and Plastics

1 Mark Questions

1. Names of some of the fibres are given below

   I. Nylon   II. Silk

   III. Lycra   IV. Polyester

   The odd one among these is

   (a) I   (b) II   (c) III   (d) IV

2. A polyester fabric should not be ironed with a hot iron because

   (a) it is a waste of electricity

   (b) the polyester will melt

   (c) the polyester will catch fire

   (d) the polyester will lose its colour

3. The first synthetic fibre, made its debut in the United States as a replacement for silk, just in time for World War II rationing is

   (a) polyester   (b) rayon

   (c) nylon   (d) spandex

4. When Rohan burnt a small piece of her mother's old (rejected) cotton saree, he got the smell of burning paper. This is because

   (a) cotton is obtained from plants

   (b) paper is obtained from plants

   (c) both cotton and paper are obtained from plants

   (d) paper is obtained from cotton plants

5. The fibres obtained from natural sources are called natural fibres and that obtained from artificial sources are called synthetic fibres.

   Here, with some fibres along with their sources are given.

	Material	Natural source	Artificial source
I.	Acrylic	✗	✓
II.	Rayon	✓	✗
III.	Nylon	✗	✓
IV.	Cellulose	✗	✓

   Key ✓ belongs to

        ✗ not belong to

   The correct matching is

   (a) I and III

   (b) II and III

   (c) III and IV

   (d) I, II and III

6. Which of the following fibre is used for making parachutes and ropes for rock climbing?

(a) Rayon　　　(b) Nylon
(c) Polyester　　(d) Acrylic

7. Which of the following fibre is a mixture of polyester and cotton?

(a) Polycot　　(b) Polywool
(c) Cotton　　(d) Wool

8. Generally, it is not advisable to wear clothes made up of terylene, nylon, etc. while bursting fire crackers.

This is because of the following reasons

I. These fibres are prepared by using raw materials of petroleum origin.

II. These fibres catch fire easily.

III. On heating, these fibres melt and get stick to the body of the person wearing it.

The correct reason(s) is/are

(a) Only I　　　(b) Only II
(c) I and III　　(d) II and III

9. Which of the following is not a natural fibre?

(a) Fibres from cocoons
(b) Fibres from fish scales
(c) Fibres from plant seeds
(d) Fibres from animal coats

10. The bristles of toothbrush are made up of nylon. Which of the following properties of nylon make it most suitable for this purpose?

I. High water absorption tendency.

II. More strength in wet condition.

III. Resistance towards bacteria and fungus.

IV. Transparency, clarity and weight.

Codes

(a) I and II　　　(b) I, II and III
(c) II and III　　(d) I and IV

11. Consider the following fabrics.

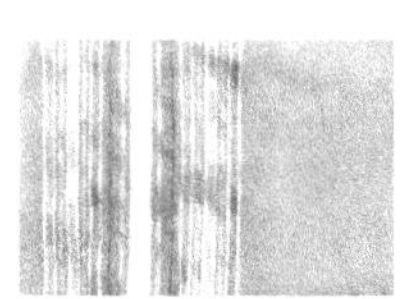

Some statements relating to these fabrics are as follows

I. They are less expensive.

II. They have combined properties of each fibre.

III. They are made by blending synthetic fibres with natural fibres.

The correct statement(s) is/are

(a) I and II　　　(b) II and III
(c) Only II　　　(d) I, II and III

12. Plastic which gets deformed easily on heating and can be bent easily is known as

(a) Thermosetting plastics
(b) Thermoplastics
(c) Both (a) and (b)
(d) Either (a) nor (b)

13. Electric plugs/switches/plug boards are made up of bakelite because of the fact that

I. It is a good conductor of heat and electricity.

II. It absorbs electric shock to save us from that.

III. It gets heated very fast.

IV. It can prevent possible fire in electrical insulations.

The correct statements are

(a) 1, III and IV
(b) I and III
(c) II and IV
(d) III and IV

14. Which of the following plastics, on which oil and water do not stick?
(a) Melamine   (b) Teflon
(c) Bakelite   (d) All of these

15. Generally, it was said that plastics are bad conductors of heat and electricity. People came to that conclusion from the following facts:
I. Plastic core is present in refrigerators or freezers.
II. Electrical wires are covered by a plastic covering.
III. Handles of cooking pans are made up of plastics.
IV. Plastics are used for making parachutes.
The correct facts are
(a) I and II   (b) I and III
(c) I. II and III   (d) I, II and IV

16. You are familiar with the following items.
I. Raincoat   II. Seat covers
In both of the above items, polymer of vinyl chloride is used. This polymer is choosed for such applications because

(a) of its lower melting point and unreactive nature
(b) of its higher melting point and very reactive nature
(c) of its tendency to get rolled into thin sheets like polythene
(d) of its tendency to get coated on a cloth base and tough nature as compared to polythene

17. Which of the following is not a common property of plastics?
(a) Non-reactive
(b) Light in weight
(c) Durable
(d) Good conductor of electricity

18. Which of the following properties would you consider, while selecting a material for storing food items?
I. It can resist high temperature.
II. It should be corrosion resistant.
III. It can be moulded into various shapes.
IV. It should not conduct heat.
Codes
(a) I and IV   (b) II and III
(c) I, II and IV   (d) All of these

2 Marks Questions

19. Match the fabrics given in Column I with their area of application (use) given in Column II and choose the correct answer using the codes given below.

	Column I		Column II
A.	Polyester	1.	Cheap silk like clothes
B.	Rayon	2.	Parachute and stocking
C.	Nylon	3.	Shrouds of Egyptian pharaohs
D.	Flax	4.	Non-wrinkable fabric

Codes

	A	B	C	D
(a)	4	1	2	3
(b)	1	4	2	3
(c)	4	1	3	2
(d)	4	3	2	1

20. Rama wants to study the effect of heating of different fibres. For this, she collected the following natural and synthetic fibres.
I. Nylon   II. Wool   III. Cotton
IV. Silk   V. Polyester

She burnt them one by one with a matchstick. After the experiment, she observed that

1. II and III burn to form a residue.
2. I and V melt on burning.
3. II and IV burn with smell of burning hair.

The true statements are

(a) 1 and 2
(b) 2 and 3
(c) 1 and 3
(d) 1, 2 and 3

21. State [T] for True and [F] for False.
    I. Silk absorbs more water than wool.
    II. Natural fibres are not resistant towards moths as well as wrinkles.
    III. Terylene, a synthetic fibre, can be used instead of wool.
    IV. Silk is the most expensive natural fibre.
    V. The capacity of fibre to withstand force is more in cotton than in nylon.

    Codes

	I	II	III	IV	V
(a)	T	T	F	F	T
(b)	T	F	T	F	T
(c)	T	T	F	T	F
(d)	F	T	F	T	F

22. Consider the following figures and related statements.

    I. P shows a monomer, whereas Q is the representation of the polymer of P.
    II. Only small circles represent the monomers that are interconnected to give a polymer.
    III. P is a linear polymer, whereas Q is a cross-linked polymer.

    The correct statements are

    (a) I and II   (b) I and III
    (c) II and III   (d) I, II and III

23. Consider the following statements about plastics.

    I. In all plastics, the arrangement of monomers is not same.
    II. Melamine is a better plastic than other to resist fire and bear heat.
    III. Some plastics have cross-linked structure.
    IV. Although, plastics are more in number but their applications are limited.

    The correct statements are

    (a) I and II   (b) II, III and II
    (c) I, II and III   (d) III and IV

Metals and Non-metals

1 Mark Questions

1. Match the properties given in Column I with the related terms given in Column II and choose the correct answer using the codes given below.

	Column I		Column II
A.	Produce ringing sound	1.	Tensile strength
B.	Can be drawn into wire	2.	Brittleness
C.	Can be beaten into sheets	3.	Sonority
D.	Can withstand the longitudinal pull	4.	Malleability
		5.	Ductility

Codes

	A	B	C	D			A	B	C	D
(a)	3	4	5	2		(b)	3	4	5	1
(c)	3	5	4	2		(d)	3	5	4	1

2. State [T] for True and [F] for False.
   I. The property of gold by virtue of which it can be drawn into wire is called its ductility.
   II. Silver is a good conductor of electricity but bad conductor of heat.
   III. Iodine is a lustrous non-metal.
   IV. Diamond is a hard non-metal which is a good conductor of heat.

   Codes

	I	II	III	IV			I	II	III	IV
(a)	T	F	F	T		(b)	T	F	T	T
(c)	T	F	T	F		(d)	F	T	F	T

3. Pots and pans used for cooking are made up of metals because
   I. metals are hard.
   II. metals are malleable.
   III. metals possess high melting point.
   IV. metals are good electrical conductors.
   V. metals are brittle.

   The correct reasons are
   (a) I, II and III
   (b) I, II, III and IV
   (c) II and IV
   (d) I and II

4. Sahil made the following experimental set up by using a copper wire.

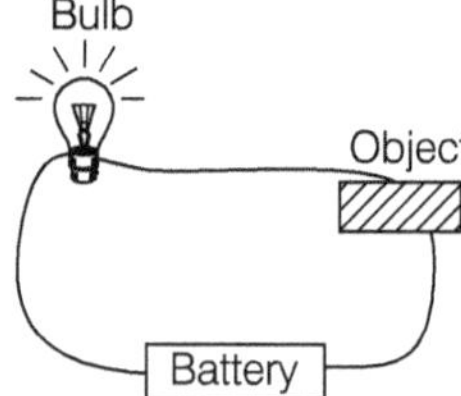

He repeated this experiment with

   I. aluminium foil

  II. iron nail

 III. coal

 IV. graphite

In which cases, the bulb will glow?

(a) I and II
(b) III and IV
(c) I, II and IV
(d) All of these

5. Mr. Verma, the science teacher, provided following information about the four samples, i.e. P, Q, R and S.

Samples	Flow of electricity	Malleability
P	✓	✗
Q	✗	✗
R	✗	✓
S	✓	✓

Key   ✓ = Possesses the property

       ✗ = Does not possess the property

Now, he told the students to identify them.

The correct identifications are

(a) P is copper and Q is sulphur
(b) Q is coal and S is copper
(c) R is iron and S is copper
(d) Q is sulphur and R is coal

6. Ravi saw his father's bicycle which was kept in the store room since a long period of time. He also noticed several red brown spots over it because of which it was not looking good. The process by which metal of the bicycle was rusted is called

(a) oxidation
(b) corrosion
(c) galvanisation
(d) amalgamation

7. Iron and steel are protected from corrosion by coating them with a layer of metals like tin, chromium, etc. We know this process by the name

(a) galvanisation
(b) painting
(c) electroplating
(d) greasing

8. Seema's grandfather filled a copper glass with water and kept it aside. He forgot about this glass. After a few days, he found a dull green coating on the glass. Seema was surprised.

Her grandfather told her that this layer contains a mixture of

(a) copper hydroxide and copper carbonate
(b) copper hydroxide and copper oxide
(c) copper oxide and copper sulphide
(d) copper sulphate and copper oxide

9. Ravi took four different materials in four different test tubes labelled as P, Q, R and S as shown below.

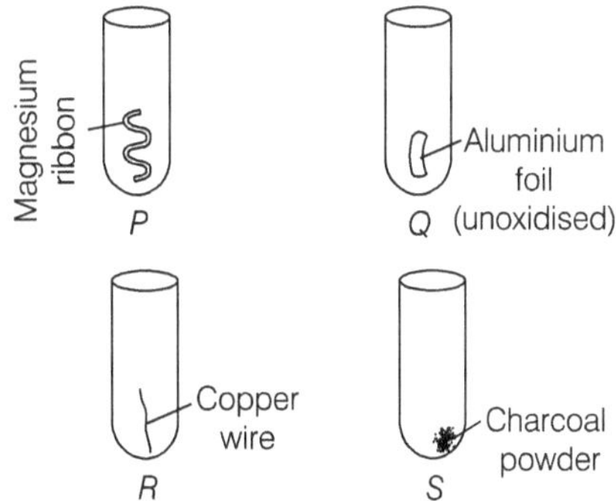

He added 5 mL dilute hydrochloric acid in each test tube and brought a burning matchstick at the mouth of each test tube. In which case(s), he will hear the pop sound?

(a) Only P
(b) P and Q
(c) Q and S
(d) P, Q and R

10. Match the substances given in Column I with their properties mentioned in Column II and choose the correct answer using the codes given below.

Column I	Column II
A. Sodium	1. Gives acidic gas when burnt
B. Phosphorus	2. No reaction with acid or base
C. Copper	3. So soft, that it can be cut with knife
D. Carbon	4. Burns spontaneously in air
	5. Turns green when exposed in air

Codes

	A	B	C	D
(a)	3	5	2	1
(b)	4	1	3	2
(c)	4	5	3	2
(d)	3	4	5	1

11. Consider the following reactions.

I. $Mg + CuSO_4 \longrightarrow MgSO_4 + Cu$

II. $Fe + ZnSO_4 \longrightarrow FeSO_4 + Zn$

III. $Ca + MgSO_4 \longrightarrow CaSO_4 + Mg$

The feasible reaction(s) is/are

(a) I and II   (b) II and III

(c) Only I   (d) I and III

12. Paheli prepared blue coloured solution of copper sulphate in beaker *A* and placed an iron nail in it. Boojho prepared a yellowish green solution of ferrous sulphate in beaker *B* and placed a copper wire in it.

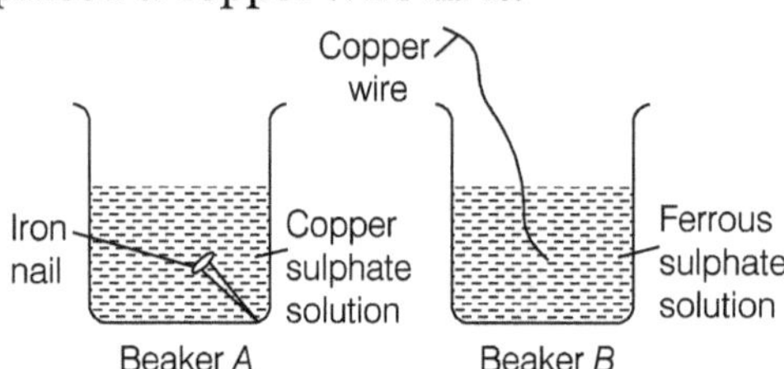

After an hour, what changes will be observed by them?

	Observation of Paheli	Observation of Boojho
(a)	No reaction	Fade green solution
(b)	Fade blue solution	No reaction
(c)	Fade blue solution	Fade green solution
(d)	No reaction	No reaction

13. Mercury is an ideal liquid for making thermometer because it

I. does not stick to glass and is easily visible.

II. expands on heating.

III. possesses high boiling point.

The correct reason(s) is/are

(a) I and II

(b) II and III

(c) Only III

(d) I, II and III

14. Match the names of the alloy given in Column I with their composition given in Column II and choose the correct answer using the codes given below.

Column I	Column II
A. Brass	1. Copper + zinc
B. Bronze	2. Iron + carbon
C. Steel	3. Copper + tin
D. Solder	4. Lead + copper
	5. Tin + lead

Codes

	A	B	C	D			A	B	C	D
(a)	1	2	4	5		(b)	2	3	4	5
(c)	1	3	2	5		(d)	1	3	2	4

15. An element contains 5 electrons in its outermost shell. Some properties in relation to it are

 I. It is a reactive metal.

 II. It is an inert element.

 III. It is non-malleable.

 IV. It is generally filled in chips packets.

The correct statement(s) is/are

(a) I and II
(b) II, III and IV
(c) I, II and III
(d) Only II

16. Consider some of the applications of aluminium metal.

 I. In making tanks and magnets.

 II. In making drink cans and foils.

 III. In making aeroplanes parts.

 IV. In making food containers and tooth filling

The incorrect applications are

(a) I and IV
(b) I, II and IV
(c) II and IV
(d) II and III

2 Marks Questions

17. Refer to the given paragraph, choose the correct option for P-S.

P is good conductor of heat and electricity whereas Q is not. R although is a non-metal but a good conductor of electricity. Metals are generally solid at room temperature whereas S is the only liquid metal. Non-metals are generally solids or gases but bromine is a liquid at room temperature.

	P	Q	R	S
(a)	Diamond	Graphite	Graphite	Gallium
(b)	Graphite	Diamond	Graphite	Gallium
(c)	Non-metal	Metal	Diamond	Mercury
(d)	Metal	Non-metal	Graphite	Mercury

18. Rama has two jars.

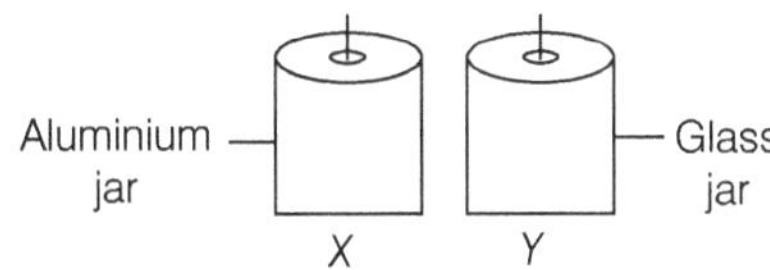

She has to store pickle in any one of them. She preferred jar Y because

 I. it does not react with pickle.

 II. it preserves the colour of the pickle.

 III. it preserves the odour of the pickle.

 IV. it preserves pickle from being spoiled.

The correct reason(s) is/are

(a) I and II
(b) I, II and III
(c) I and IV
(d) Only I

19. Aparna took a sample of substance X and burnt it in the following assembly.

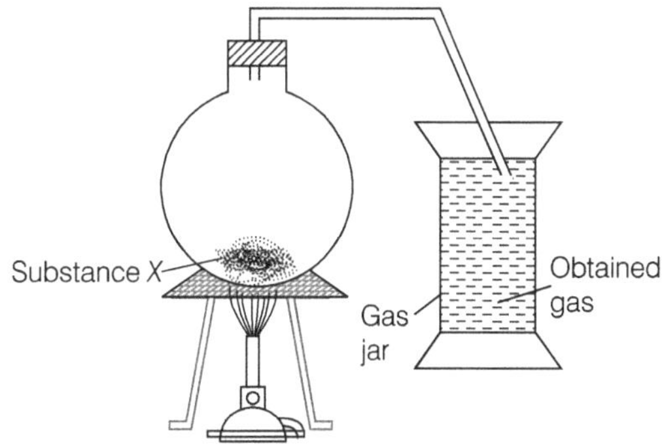

After the reaction, she tested the obtained gas by using solution of calcium hydroxide in water. She observed that the solution turns milky. It suggests that the substance burnt by her was a

(a) metal
(b) non-metal
(c) metalloid
(d) Data insufficient

20. Consider the following statements.

I. Metal X can displace Y from its salt solution but not hydrogen from water or dilute acid.

II. Metals Z and A both release hydrogen with dilute acids.

III. Metal Z releases hydrogen with nitric acid but metal A does not.

IV. Metal A is not able to displace metal Z from its salt solution.

On the basis of above observations, the order of reactivity of these metals is

(a) $Z > A > X > Y$
(b) $A > Z > X > Y$
(c) $Z > A > Y > X$
(d) $A > Z > Y > X$

21. Some of the points of difference between metals and non-metals are given below.

S. No.	Property	Metals	Non-metals
I.	Reaction with oxygen	Basic oxides are obtained	Acidic oxides are obtained
II.	Reaction with salt of less reactive element	Displacement takes place	Displacement takes place

S. No.	Property	Metals	Non-metals
III.	Reaction with water	Hydrogen is evolved	No reaction takes place
IV.	Reaction with dilute acids	A gas with pop sound evolves	No reaction takes place

The correct points are

(a) II, III and IV
(b) I, II and III
(c) I, III and IV
(d) I, II, III and IV

22. Consider the following statements.

I. On burning, metals react with oxygen to produce metal oxides, which are basic in nature.

II. On burning, metals react with oxygen to produce metal oxides, which are acidic in nature.

III. On burning, non-metals react with oxygen to produce non-metallic oxides which are basic in nature.

IV. On burning, there is reaction of non-metals with oxygen.

The incorrect statements are

(a) I and II
(b) I, II and III
(c) II and III
(d) II and IV

Chapter 05

Coal and Petroleum

1 Mark Questions

1. Consider the following states of carbon.

   I. Coke   II. Charcoal
III. Petrol   IV. Graphite

Which of these are considered as free states of carbon?

(a) I and II   (b) II and III
(c) I, II and III   (d) I, II and IV

2. Consider the following statements about exhaustible natural resources.

Statement I Limited in quantity.

Statement II Not dependent on nature.

Statement III Exhausted by human activities.

The correct statements are

(a) I and II   (b) II and III
(c) I and III   (d) I, II and III

3. Match the distillation product of coal given in Column I with their preparation/applications given in Column II and choose the correct answer using the codes given below.

	Column I		Column II
A.	Coke	1.	Remains of vegetation
B.	Coal tar	2.	Fuel
C.	Coal gas	3.	Synthesis of plastics, paints, etc
D.	Coal	4.	Extraction of metals

Codes

	A	B	C	D			A	B	C	D
(a)	1	3	2	4		(b)	4	3	2	1
(c)	4	2	3	1		(d)	1	2	3	4

4. Which of the following product is formed after complete combustion of methane?

(a) Carbon dioxide (b) Carbon monoxide
(c) Charcoal   (d) Carbon

5. Consider the following actions while driving.

  I. Switch off engine at traffic lights.
 II. Ensure correct tyre pressure.
III. Maintain vehicle well from time to time.

Which will help in saving petrol?

(a) I and II   (b) II and III
(c) Only III   (d) I, II and III

6. State [T] for True and [F] for False.

  I. Bitumen is obtained from coal tar.
 II. Wildlife is an example of exhaustible natural resource.
III. Bitumen is used for surfacing roads.
VI. Carbonisation is a fast process.

Codes

	I	II	III	IV			I	II	III	IV
(a)	F	T	T	F		(b)	F	T	F	T
(c)	T	F	F	T		(d)	T	F	T	F

7. Rohan saw a bucket filled with some black liquid.

When he went near the liquid, he felt some unpleasant odour, The engineer working there tell him that this substance is a mixture of 200 substances.

On the basis of information provided above, could you guess what was that substance?

(a) Coke   (b) Coal
(c) Coal tar   (d) Coal gas

8. Coal is processed in industries to get some useful products. Some products that are supposed to be obtained from the coal are

  I. Coke   II. Coal gas
III. Coal tar   IV. CNG

The correct products are

(a) I and II   (b) I and III
(c) I, II and III   (d) I, II, III and IV

9. Substance X is obtained by processing coal and was used for street lighting in 1810 or 1820. It is used for the preparation of

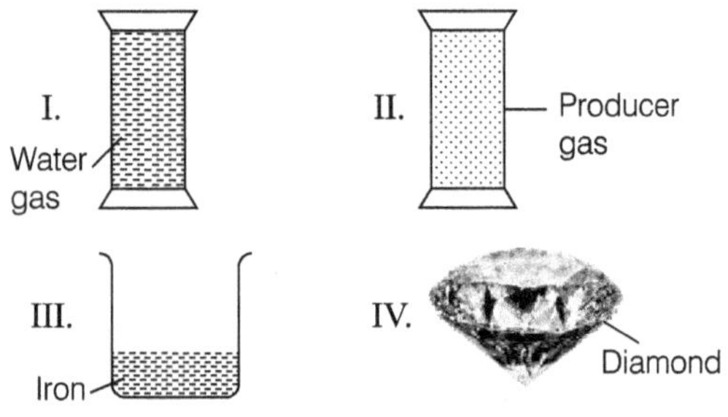

(a) I and II   (b) I, II and IV
(c) I, III and IV   (d) Only IV

10. Consider the following statements.

  I. Slow conversion of dead vegetation into fossil fuel.
 II. Slow conversion of fossil fuels into coal.

III. Process occurring at very high temperature and pressure.

The true statement(s) regarding carbonisation is/are

(a) I and III   (b) II and III
(c) Only I   (d) Only III

11. Several materials can be obtained from coal tar, some of them are mentioned below.

  I. Naphthalene balls   II. Perfumes
III. Drugs   IV. Cookware
  V. Fuel
VI. Extracted metal

The correct materials are

(a) I and III   (b) I, II and III
(c) II, III and IV   (d) IlI, IV and VI

12. Match the varieties of coal given in Column I with their carbon content/property given in Column II and choose the correct alternative using the codes given below.

	Column I		Column II
A.	Lignite	1.	Most common variety
B.	Anthracite	2.	60% carbon
C.	Peat	3.	30% carbon
D.	Bituminous	4.	Purest variety
		5.	Brown coal

Codes

	A	B	C	D		A	B	C	D
(a)	5	4	2	1	(b)	5	4	3	1
(c)	4	1	2	3	(d)	5	1	3	4

13. In homework, Ravi's teacher gave him an assignment for writing one word for the following substances.

  I. A mixture of about 200 substances.
 II. A porous, black, almost pure form of carbon.
III. A fossil fuel used in thermal power plants for generating electricity.

Could you help Ravi in identifying 1, II and III?

	I	II	III
(a)	Coke	Coal gas	Petroleum
(b)	Coal tar	Coke	Coal
(c)	Coke	Coal tar	Coal
(d)	Coal tar	Coal	Coal gas

14. Which of the following sources of energy can be a good alternative of coal in a power station?

   I. Geothermal energy

  II. Energy from water

 III, Energy from petrol

 IV. Energy from plants

(a) I and II   (b) 1,II and III

(c) Only IV   (d) 1, I1, III and IV

15. Consider the following statements.

   I. Coal is made up of only carbon.

  II. Anthracite and lignite are the two main types of coal.

 III. Anthracite coal is the hardest and has more çarbon content.

 IV. Lignite is the softest and has high carbon and oxygen content.

The incorrect statements are

(a) I and III   (b) 1,II and II

(c) 1, II and IV   (d) I1, III and IV

16. Petroleum is deposited with gas in the rocks known as oil wells from where it is taken out by drilling. In these wells, the petroleum and gas are found in the layer X-water because they are Y-than water.

	X	Y
(a)	Below	Heavier
(b)	Above	Lighter
(c)	Between	Of equal weight
(d)	Similar to	Of equal weight

17. Consider the following statements about natural gas.

   I. It is difficult to transport it through pipes.

  II. It cannot be used directly for burning in homes.

 III. It is stored under high pressure as compressed nátural gas.

 IV. It cannot be used for power generation.

The incorrect statements are

(a) I and II

(b) III andIV

(c) I, II and III

(d) I, II and IV

18. Which of the following are the constituents of petroleum?

(a) Diesel, paraffin

(b) CNG, coal tar

(c) Coal tar, bitumen

(d) Kerosene, coal gas

19. Match the items given in Column I with the items given in Column II and choose the correct answer using the codes given below:

	Column I		Column II
A.	Petroleum gas in liquid form	1.	Black gold
B.	Natural gas	2.	LPG
C.	Petroleum	3.	CNG
D.	Paraffin wax	4.	Bitumen
		5.	Vaseline

Codes

	A	B	C	D
(a)	2	3	1	4
(b)	4	3	1	5
(c)	2	3	1	5
(d)	3	2	5	1

20. When subjected to fractional distillation, petroleum gives different fractions, some of which are mentioned below.

   I. Petroleum gas   II. Lubricating oil
III. Kerosene   IV. Gasoline

What is the correct sequence of these fractions in the fractionating column from top to bottom?

(a) I. I1. III, IV   (b) III, I, II, IV
(c) I, IV, III, II   (d) IV, III, I, II

21. State [T] for True and [F] for False.

   I. Natural gas can be supplied to homes and factories through pipes.
  II. Natural gas is obtained by fractional distillation of crude oil.
 III. Natural gas is a cleaner fuel because on burning only water is produced.
 IV. Natural gas is an exhaustible source of energy like fossil fuels.

Codes

	I	II	III	IV			I	II	III	IV
(a)	T	F	T	T	(b)		T	T	F	T
(c)	F	T	T	F	(d)		F	F	T	F

22. Consider the following statements.

   I. During the fractional distillation of petroleum, hydrocarbons having highest boiling point condenses first.
  II. Petrochemicals are those useful substances that are obtained from petroleum and natural gas.
 III. Paraffin wax is used in making candles, vaseline, polish, etc.

The correct statements are

(a) I and II   (b) II and III
(c) I and III   (d) I,II and III

23. When petroleum is subjected to fractional distillation, a fraction X, lies in between the petrol and diesel oil is obtained. This fraction is used

   I. as a fuel for stoves and lamps.
  II. in paints and motor fuel.
 III. in jet fuel.

The correct use (s) is/are

(a) I and II
(b) I and III
(c) II and III
(d) Only I

2 Marks Questions

24. Complete the following sentence by selecting the most appropriate set of words.

X is an exhaustible natural resource which is found in Y quantity in nature and is Z likely to get exhausted by human activities.

	X	Y	Z
(a)	Coal	limited	always
(b)	Air	unlimited	most
(c)	Sunlight	unlimited	never
(d)	Petroleum	unlimited	never

25. Coal is a fossil fuel and it cannot be prepared in the laboratory or industry because its preparation

   I. is a very slow process.
  II. occurs only at a very low temperature and pressure.
 III. requires very high temperature and pressure,
 IV. is a great source of pollution

The correct reasons are

(a) 1 and II   (b) II and IV
(c) I and III   (d) II, I and IV

26. Consider the following statements
    I. Oil and natural gas are found under the ground between folds of rock in the porous areas.
    I1. In search of oil and natural gas, companies drill through the earth to the deposits deep below the surface.
    III. The oil and natural gas are then pumped from the ground by oil rigs.
    IV. The petroleum or crude oil can be used in the same state in which it is found.

    The correct statements are
    (a) I and II (b) I, II and III
    (c) II, III and IV (b) II and II

27. State [T] for True and [F] for False.
    I. Wildlife is an exhaustible natural resource.
    II. Methane is released during mining of coal.
    III. Fossil fuels should be conserved because they give out lots of heat.
    IV. Resources that are present in unlimited quantity in nature are called exhaustible natural resources.
    V. Burning of coal in insufficient amount of oxygen results in the formation of carbon dioxide.

    Codes

	I	II	III	IV	V
(a)	T	T	F	T	F
(b)	F	T	T	F	F
(c)	T	T	F	F	F
(d)	T	F	F	F	F

Chapter 06

Combustion and Flame

1 Mark Questions

1. Combustion takes place only when
   I. oxygen/air is available.
   II. air/oxygen and fuel are available.
   II. temperature of the fuel is lower than ignition temperature.
   IV. temperature of the fuel is above the ignition temperature.

   The correct statements are
   (a) I and II   (b) II and IV
   (c) I and III   (d) I and IV

2. Some processes are given below
   I. Burning of candle
   II. Burning of wood
   III. Burning of paper

   From these, the example(s) of slow combustion is/are
   (a) Only II
   (b) Only III
   (c) II and III
   (d) I, II and III

3. Consider the following experiment.

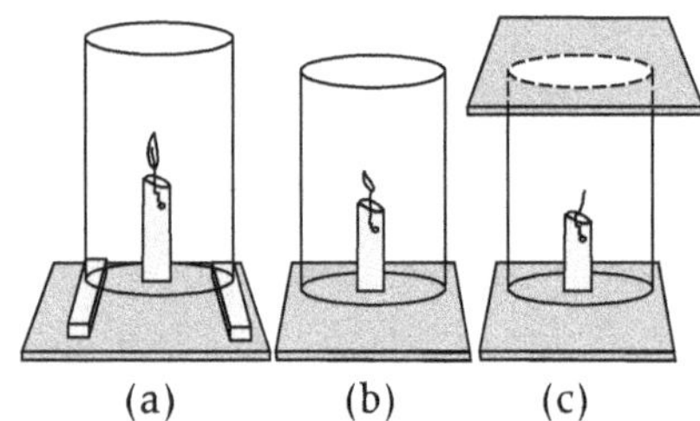

This experiment shows that
(a) candle can burn in a glass chimney
(b) candle cannot burn in a glass chimney
(c) wood is essential for combustion
(d) oxygen is essential for combustion

4. Consider the following statements.
   I. Sulphur burns in air at room temperature.
   II. Most fires occur due to human carelessness.
   III. During rapid combustion, a material suddenly bursts into flame.
   IV. Spontaneous combustion of coal dust has led to forest fires.

   The correct statements are
   (a) I and II   (b) II and III
   (c) II and IV   (d) II and IV

5. Consider the following diagram.

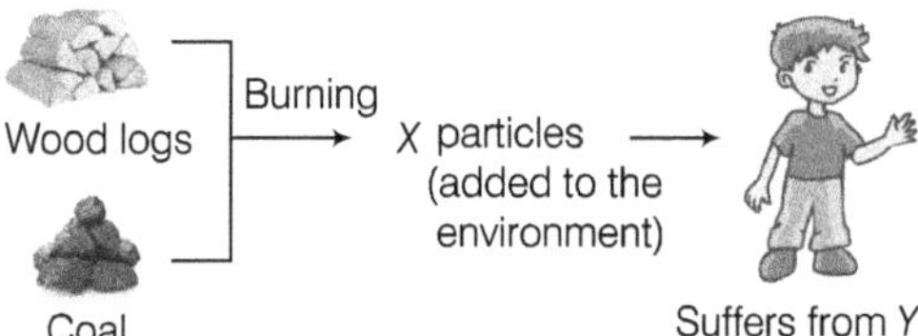

Here, X and Y are
(a) burnt carbon, respiratory disease
(b) burnt carbon, nervous disease
(c) unburnt carbon, respiratory disease
(d) unburnt carbon, stomach disease

6. Match the processes given in Column I with their combustion type given in Column II and choose the correct answer using the codes given below.

	Column I		Column II
A.	Burning of candle	1.	Explosion
B.	Burning of phosphorus	2.	Slow combustion
C.	Burning of LPG	3.	Incomplete combustion
D.	Burning of crackers	4.	Spontaneous combustion
		5.	Rapid combustion

Codes

	A	B	C	D
(a)	2	3	4	1
(b)	2	4	3	1
(c)	2	4	5	1
(d)	2	4	1	5

7. State [T] for True and [F] for False and choose correct option.

I. Fire extinguishers extinguish the fire by bringing down the temperature of fuel.

II. The heat and light produced by Sun are also the result of combustion process.

III. Fire can be controlled by removing one or more factors essential for its production.

IV. Ignition temperature is very low for inflammable substances.

Codes

	I	II	III	IV
(a)	F	F	T	T
(b)	T	T	F	F
(c)	F	T	T	F
(d)	F	F	F	T

8. Consider the following figures.

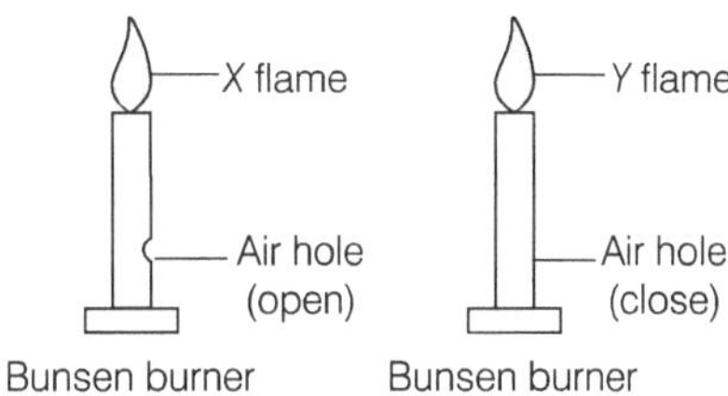

Here, X and Y respectively are
(a) blue and green   (b) yellow and blue
(c) yellow and green (d) blue and yellow

9. State [T] for True and [F] for False.

I. In luminous zone of a candle, partial combustion takes place with the evolution of large quantity of heat energy.

II. Middle zone is the hottest part of the flame.

III. All the fuels burn with flame.

IV. Kerosene oil and molten wax produce flame.

Codes

	I	II	III	IV		I	II	III	IV
(a)	F	T	T	F	(b)	F	F	T	F
(c)	F	T	T	T	(d)	F	F	F	T

10. Ramesh wants to test the hotness of different parts of the flame. For this, he took a beaker filled with water and heat it in

I. non-luminous zone.   II. dark zone.

III. luminous zone.

He recorded the time taken by the same amount of water to reach a temperature of 50°C and make the following table.

Zone	Volume of water taken	Time taken to reach 50°C
I	20 mL	15 min
II	20 mL	10 min
III	20 mL	20 min

The incorrect observation(s) is/are
(a) Only III   (b) II and III
(c) Only II   (d) Only I

11. In case of good fuels, ignition temperature is X and calorific value is Y. X and Y respectively are
(a) low and high   (b) low and low
(c) high and low   (d) high and high

12. Match the pollutants given in Column I with their harmful effects given in Column II and choose the correct answer using the codes given below.

	Column I		Column II
A.	Smoke	1.	Greenhouse effect
B.	Carbon monoxide	2.	Lung diseases
C.	Dust	3.	Allergic reaction
D.	Oxides of nitrogen	4.	Chocking of throat
		5.	Respiratory problems

Codes

	A	B	C	D			A	B	C	D
(a)	5	3	2	1		(b)	5	4	3	2
(c)	4	3	2	1		(d)	5	3	4	2

13. In an experiment, 4.5 kg of a fuel was completely burnt. During this process, the heat produced was 180000 kJ.

The calorific value of the fuel (in kJ/kg) is
(a) 10000 (b) 20000 (c) 40000 (d) 80000

14. Global warming is a serious environmental problem which leads to the rise in sea level resulting in floods in coastal areas.

The cause of global warming is
(a) sulphur dioxide released by combustion of fuels and resulting in increased temperature

(b) carbon monoxide added to the environment due to combustion of fuel and result in decreased temperature
(c) carbon dioxide added to the environment due to combustion of fuel and resulting in increased temperature
(d) None of the above

15. Consider the consequences of green house effect.

   I. Existence of life on the Earth.

  II. Melting of ice on the Earth's pole.

 III. Floods on low lying areas of the Earth.

 IV. Warmth of the Earth.

The correct statements are
(a) I and IV   (b) II and III
(c) I, II and III   (d) All of these

16. If A is hydrogen, which property of A prevents it from becoming an ideal fuel?
(a) Its highest calorific value
(b) Its very low ignition temperature
(c) Its very high solubility in water
(d) Its pollution free nature as the byproduct formed after combustion is also important for existence of life.

17. In the following Venn diagram.

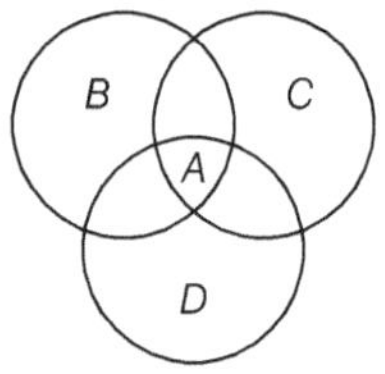

Identify A, B, C and D.

	A	B	C	D
(a)	Natural fuels	Wood	Coal	Cowdung cake
(b)	Fossil fuels	Wood	Coal	Petroleum
(c)	Natural fuels	Petroleum	Wood	Coal
(d)	Fossil fuels	Cowdung cake	Wood	Petroleum

2 Marks Questions

18. Sometimes, rainwater is found harmful for crops, buildings, soil, etc. Such rain is called acid rain and is responsible for the decolouration of Taj Mahal over years. The main cause of acid rain is

(a) release of carbon monoxide due to incomplete combustion of fuel, which dissolves in rainwater to give acid rain

(b) release of carbon particles in the atmosphere which dissolve in rainwater to give acid rain

(c) release of oxides of sulphur and nitrogen during the combustion of fuel, which dissolve in rainwater to give acid rain

(d) release of methane and other gases due to burning of wood, which dissolve in rainwater to give acid rain

19. State [T] for True and [F] for False.

I. Magnesium is a non-combustible metal.

II. A physical process in which a substance reacts with oxygen to give off heat is called combustion.

III. Alcohol, CNG and LPG are inflammable substances.

IV. Carbon dioxide is an excellent fire extinguisher.

V. At airport and petrol pump, soda-acid fire extinguishers are not used.

Codes

	I	II	III	IV	V
(a)	F	F	T	F	T
(b)	F	F	T	T	T
(c)	F	T	T	T	F
(d)	T	F	F	T	T

20. Match the items given in Column I with their most suitable match given in Column II and choose the correct answer using the codes given below.

	Column I		Column II
A.	Rapid combustion	1.	Material burns without any apparent cause
B.	Explosion	2.	Fire extinguishers
C.	Baking soda	3.	Material burns with only sound but no heat or lig.ht
D.	Spontaneous combustion	4.	Evolution of large amount of heat, light and sound
		5.	Material burns rapidly to give heat and light

Codes

	A	B	C	D		A	B	C	D
(a)	5	4	1	2	(b)	5	4	2	1
(c)	5	3	2	1	(d)	4	5	1	3

21. When a candle burns in air, following two changes take place.

Change A and change B.

Some of the statements about change A and change B are given below.

I. Change A is a chemical change.

II. Change B is a reversible change.

III. Both change A and change B are irreversible.

The correct statement(s) is/are

(a) Only I   (b) I and II

(c) I and III   (d) Only III

Conservation of Plants and Animals

1 Mark Questions

1. Animal X is at an extremely high risk of becoming extinct. Such animals are labelled in Red Data Book as
   (a) endangered
   (b) vulnerable
   (c) extinct
   (d) critically endangered

2. Identify the incorrectly matched pair of protected areas and the species being protected
   (a) Jim Corbett National Park—Tigers
   (b) Kaziranga National Park—Tigers
   (c) Gir National Park—Asiatic Lion
   (d) Mudumalai Sanctuary—Indian elephant

3. Which of the following is an incorrect match?

   (a) 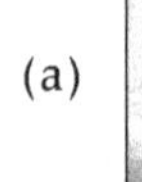 Endemic

   (b) 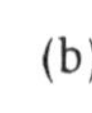 Extinct

   (c)  Threatened

   (d) 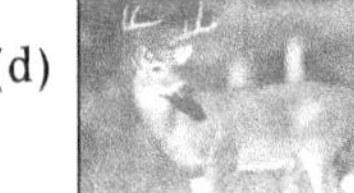 Endangered

4. In some countries, the buying and selling of animals such as orangutans and leatherback turtles have been banned. These animals need to be protected so that
   (a) their value can increase
   (b) their numbers can increase
   (c) the zoos can attract more visitors
   (d) scientists can have more animals for experiments

5. I was a large heavy flightless bird. I was hunted in large number in the island of Madagascar. The last member of my species died in 1680, who am I?

   (a) Broad billed duck
   (b) Dodo
   (c) The great Indian bustard
   (d) Grey jungle fowl

6. Would a city like Mumbai be greatly affected by deforestation? What would be the effects of deforestation on a large urban city?
   (a) No, it would not be affected, it is too far from the forests.
   (b) Yes, it would be affected, there would be scarcity of water and resources got from forests, air pollution would also increase.
   (c) No, cities are independent and do not need forests for any purpose.
   (d) Yes, animals who have lost their habitat would come to the cities in search of food.

7. Read the characteristics of two methods of biodveristy conservation.

P	Q
A man-made place for animals.	Animals live in their natural habitat. It is not man-made.
The animals are kept in artificial setting instead of their natural habitat and provided protection.	It provides protection and suitable living conditions to wild animals just like in their natural habitat.

Select the option which correctly identifies *P* and *Q*.

	P	Q
(a)	Wildlife sanctuary	Biosphere reserve
(b)	Zoo	National parks
(c)	Zoo	Wildlife sanctuary
(d)	Wildlife sanctuary	Botanical gardens

8. Read the given statements and select the correct option.

   Statement I A plant or animal species which is exclusively found in a particular area and is not found naturally anywhere else, is known as endemic species.

   Statement II The existence of endemic species is often threatened due to the introduction of exotic species from some other geographical area.
   (a) Both statements I and II are correct
   (b) Both statements I and II are incorrect
   (c) Statement I is correct and statement II is incorrect
   (d) Statement I is incorrect and statement II is correct

9. Which of these actions should be adopted by us to save the environment?
   I. We can plant trees in open spaces, parks and alongside road.
   II. We can recycle our organic waste from kitchen for making compost and use it in our kitchen garden for growing plants.
   III. We can save, reuse and recycle paper.
   IV. We can keep birds and animals in our house.
      Choose the correct option.
   (a) I, II and IV   (b) I, II and III
   (c) I, III and IV   (d) I, II, III and IV

2 Marks Questions

10. Which of the following is not a consequence of deforestation in an area?

   I. Increase in CO_2 levels.

  II. Increased rainfall.

 III. Increase in groundwater levels.

 IV. Soil erosion.

  V. Habitat destruction.

 VI. Increased temperature and pollution.

VII. Decreased flood and droughts.

VIII. Desertification.

Codes

(a) I, II and III   (b) IV, V and VIII

(c) II, III and VII (d) I, IV, V, VI and VIII

11. Migratory birds like Siberian cranes fly to far away areas like Bharatpur sanctuary in Rajasthan every year during a particular time.

Which of the following conditions of their habitats is responsible for migratory habits of birds?

  (i) Unavailability of food.

 (ii) Extremely cold weather conditions.

(iii) Lack of nesting (egg laying) areas.

(iv) Overcrowding of their habitats.

(a) (i) and (ii)   (b) (ii) and (iii)

(c) (iii) and (iv)   (d) (i), (ii) and (iv)

12. Project Tiger is an initiative for tiger conservation, started in 1972-73 in India. From the box given below, identify the names associated with this project.

> Sunderbans, Bharatpur sanctuary, Manas sanctuary, Bandipur National Park, Great Himalayan National Park, Jim Corbett National Park, Indian Botanical Garden.

Select the correct option.

(a) 4   (b) 5   (c) 3   (d) 2

13. Arrange in order, the process that leads to desertification.

(a) Soil erosion → fewer trees → removal of top layer of soil → less fertility, less humus → desertification

(b) Fewer trees → removal of top layer of soil → less fertility, less humus → soil erosion → desertification

(c) Removal of top layer of soil → fewer trees → soil erosion → less fertility, less humus → desertification

(d) Fewer trees → soil erosion → removal of top layer of soil → less fertility, less humus → desertification

14. The given below organism is not found in present era but many skeletons or fossils of these animals are found in different places of Earth providing an evidence that they were present on the Earth thousands of years ago. What would be the reason/s that these organisms have disappeared from the world?

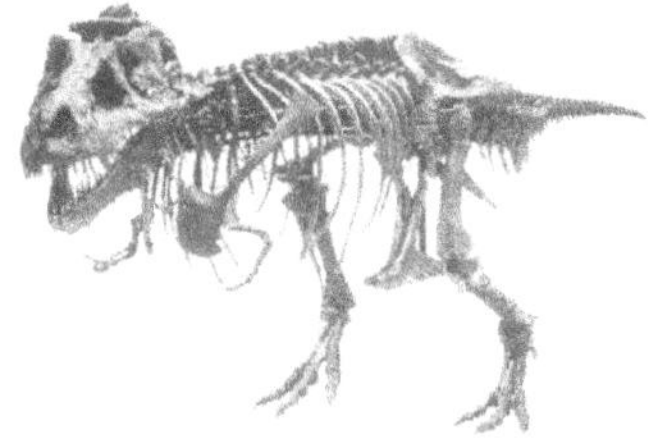

   I. These animals were threatened or killed by other animals in abundance.

  II. They were dependent on other organisms for their food.

 III. The environmental conditions made their survival harder on Earth.

 IV. They were not herbivores.

Select the correct option.

(a) Only I   (b) Only II

(c) III and IV   (d) II and III

Cell: Structures and Functions

1 Mark Questions

1. I am an animal cell that needs to travel fast from one part to another in an organism.
   I am able to travel through small spaces quickly because I do not have a nucleus. My function is to distribute a gas. Which cell am I?
   (a) White blood cell (b) Red blood cell
   (c) Nerve cell (d) Egg cell

2. Which of the following sets contains unicellular organisms only?
   (a) *Paramecium, Bougainvillea*
   (b) *Euglena, Chlorella, Chlamydomonas*
   (c) *Euglena, Saccharomyces*, Dog.
   (d) *Rhizopus, Spirogyra, Solanum*

3. The figure given below represents a X cell which is involved in Y. Select the option which is correct for X and Y.

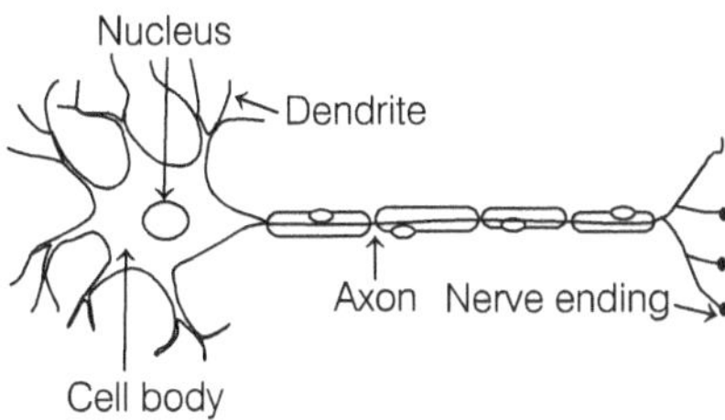

	X	Y
(a)	Cardiac muscle cell	Beating of heart
(b)	Red blood cells	Transport of gases
(c)	Neuron	Transmit neural impulses
(d)	Sperm	Helps in reproduction

4. X, Y and Z are different organisms. X is a multicellular eukaryote, Y is a unicellular eukaryote, while Z is an organism which is prokaryote. What can be X, Y and Z?

	X	Y	Z
(a)	Mould	*Euglena*	Giraffe
(b)	Human	Yeast	*E. coli*
(c)	Balsam plant	*E. coli*	Algae
(d)	*Amoeba*	Bacteria	Moss

5. In a dog, the organisation consist of the following

1. Organ system   2. Tissues
3. Organs   4. Organism
5. Cells

Arrange them in sequence from simplest to the most complex and choose the correct option.
(a) $5 \rightarrow 2 \rightarrow 3 \rightarrow 1 \rightarrow 4$
(b) $4 \rightarrow 1 \rightarrow 3 \rightarrow 2 \rightarrow 5$
(c) $5 \rightarrow 1 \rightarrow 2 \rightarrow 3 \rightarrow 4$
(d) $4 \rightarrow 3 \rightarrow 2 \rightarrow 1 \rightarrow 5$

6. Which of the following pairs are incorrectly matched?
(a) Cell theory—Schleiden and Schwann
(b) PPLO—Smallest cell in the living world
(c) Discovery of cell—Kolliker
(d) Longest cell in body—Neuron

7. Assertion (A) The size of the cells of an elephant will not be bigger than that of rat's cells.

Reason (R) The size of a cell is independent of body size.

Which of the following statement is correct?
(a) Both A and R are true and R is the correct explanation of A
(b) Both A and R are true, but R is not the correct explanation of A
(c) A is true, but R is false
(d) R is true, but A is false

8. Study the given below flow chart and mark which of the following descriptions is best suited for *A* and *B*.

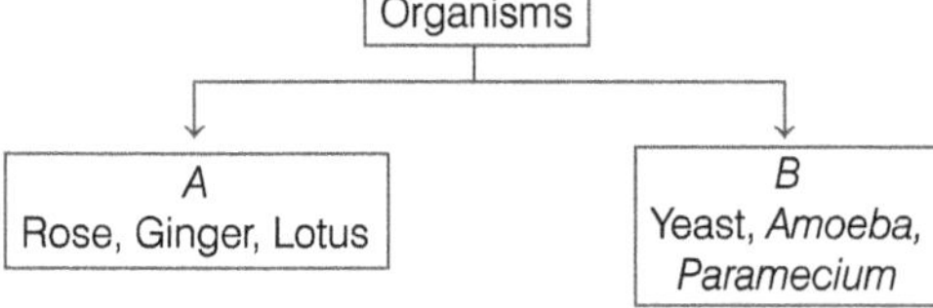

	A	B
(a)	Live in gardens	Live in forests
(b)	Living things	Non-living things
(c)	Have many cells	Have one cell
(d)	Can respond to changes	Cannot respond to changes

9. Study the plant cell below.

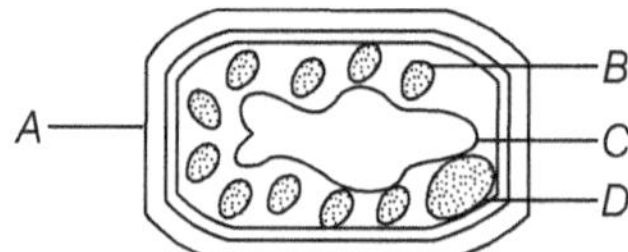

Which label part provides protection against environmental changes and injury?
(a) *B*   (b) *D*   (c) *D*   (d) *A*

10. When a red stain is added to a culture containing both living and dead cells, only the dead cells take up the stain.

Which of the following structure prevents the stain entering the living cells?
(a) Cell membrane
(b) Cytoplasm
(c) Cell wall
(d) Vacuole

11. Locate the part, which controls all the activities performed by the cell.

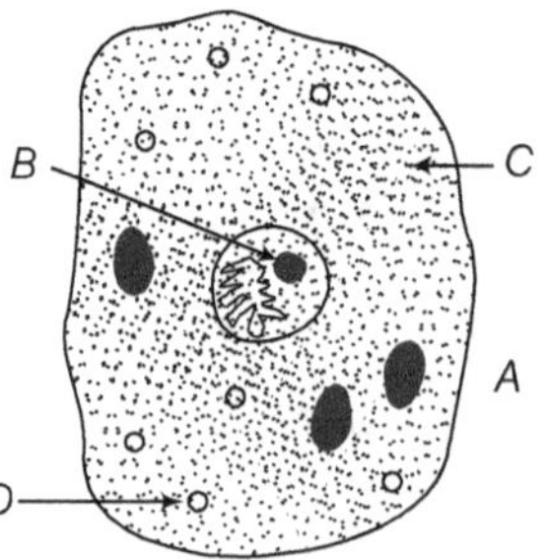

Codes
(a) *C*   (b) *A*
(c) *B*   (d) *D*

12. In animal and plant cells, the kitchen is
(a) Golgi body and endoplasmic reticulum, respectively
(b) mitochondria and Golgi body, respectively
(c) chloroplast and endoplasmic reticulum, respectively
(d) mitochondria and chloroplast, respectively

13. Observe the figure given below.

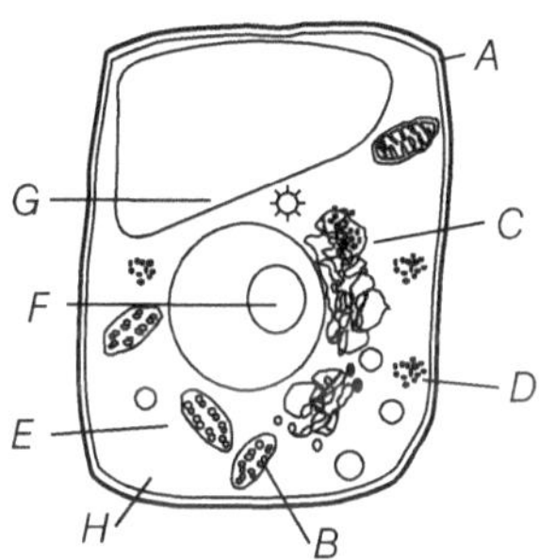

A student has identified the above cell as that of a plant. The presence of which labelled parts will confirm that the cell is a plant cell?
(a) *A*, *B* and *G*
(b) *E*, *F* and *H*
(c) *C*, *D*, *F* and *G*
(d) All of the above

14. Which of the option correctly mark the structures present in animal cells?
Key
✓ = structure present
✗ = structure absent

	Cell membrane	Cell wall	Chloroplasts	Cytoplasm
(a)	✗	✓	✓	✓
(b)	✓	✗	✗	✓
(c)	✓	✗	✓	✗
(d)	✓	✓	✗	✓

15. Read the characteristics of an organelle *X* present in our cells.
- It is spherical or rod-shaped organelle.
- Double membraned.
- Inner membrane is folded multiple times to form a series of projection called *Y*.
- Major function is energy production.
- The *X* and *Y* are correctly identified as

> i. chloroplasts, ii. thylackoids, iii. mitochondria, iv. cristae, v. endoplasmic reticulum, vi. ribosomes

(a) i and ii   (b) iii and iv
(c) v and vi   (d) iv and v

16. Which of the following could represent '*X*'?

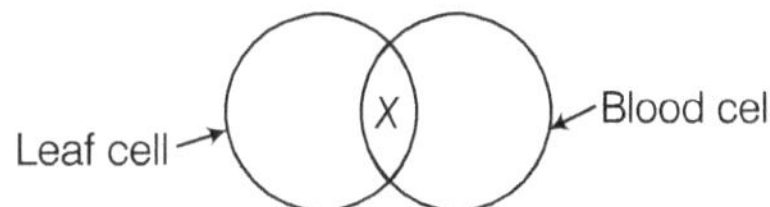

A. Nucleus   B. Mitochondria
C. Cell wall   D. Chloroplast
(a) A, B and C
(b) A, B and D
(c) A and B
(d) C and D

2 Marks Questions

17. Match the Column I with Column II.

	Column I		Column II
A.	Ribosomes	1.	Protein factories
B.	Golgi complex	2.	Cell division
C.	Cell wall	3.	Protein synthesis
D.	Centrosome	4.	Suicidal bags
E.	Lysosome	5.	Cellulose

Codes

	A	B	C	D	E
(a)	3	1	5	2	4
(b)	1	3	5	2	4
(c)	1	3	5	4	2
(d)	3	1	2	5	4

18. Rohini's younger sister studies in class VIII. One day Rohini asked her a question to check her knowledge. She wrote few statements about an organism as given below

I. Organism is an animal.

II. It feeds on other organisms.

III. It needs energy to stay alive.

IV. It can be seen with naked eyes.

Reading it, her younger sister at once told that it is a multicellular organism.

Which of the statement(s) was/were used to conclude that organisms is made up of many cells?

(a) Only III

(b) I and IV

(c) II and III

(d) I, II, III and IV

19. Complete the table given below.

Year	Scientist	Discovery
1665	…A…	Observed dead plant cells.
…B	…C…	Plants are made up of cells.
1839	…D…	Animals are made up of cells.

Identify the appropriate term to fill the blanks from the box below and select the correct option.

> I. Robert Brown, II. 1674, III. Schwann, IV. 1838, V. Robert Hooke, VI. Leeuwenhoek VII. Schleiden, IX. JE Purkinje, X. R Virchow

	A	B	C	D
(a)	I	II	III	VI
(b)	VI	II	IX	X
(c)	X	IV	V	I
(d)	V	IV	VII	III

20. The given diagram shows a group of animal cells.

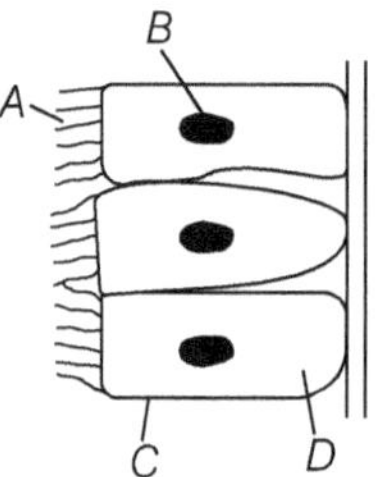

Complete the table by matching each of the functions described to a cell part *A-B*.

	Function	Cell part
I.	Controls cell activities and development	......
II.	Contains cell organelles and is the site of chemical reactions	......
III.	Waft mucus and bacteria away from the lungs	......
IV.	Controls what substances enter and leave the cell	......

Codes

	I	II	III	IV		I	II	III	IV
(a)	B	D	A	C	(b)	D	B	A	C
(c)	A	B	D	C	(d)	C	D	A	B

21. In the figure of a plant cell shown below, Identify the parts labelled X and Y based on the characteristics/functions listed below.

A. X helps in lipid biosynthesis.

B. Y maintains water balance and provides turgidity to cell.

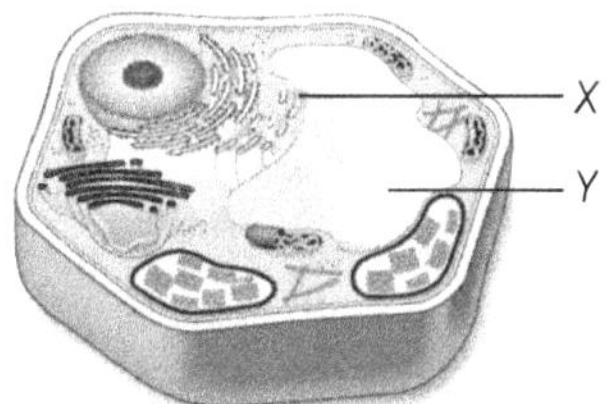

Select the correct option.

I. X could be endoplasmic reticulum.

II. Y could be chloroplast.

III. X could be mitochondria where energy related products are present.

IV. Y could be single vacuole filled with cell sap.

V. X could be the site of photosynthesis.

Codes

(a) I and V

(b) II and IV

(c) I and IV

(d) III and IV

22. From the list given below in the box, identify the correct ones to fill the table that follows

1. Cell wall,	2. Chloroplast,
3. Chromosomes,	4. Leucoplast,
5. Mitochondria,	6. Nucleus,
7. Cell membrane,	8. Vacuoles

	Description of cell	Missing part of cell
A.	Cell loses its regular shape	......
B.	Cell has no control over its activities	......
C.	Cell is unable to control what passes into and out of cell	......
D.	Cell is unable to make its own food	......

Codes

	A	B	C	D
(a)	8	5	7	4
(b)	1	6	7	2
(c)	1	3	7	8
(d)	7	6	1	2

Reproduction in Animals

1 Mark Questions

1. In which part of the female reproductive system does a fertilised egg normally develop into a baby?

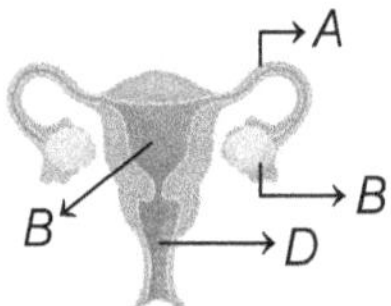

   (a) C (b) A (c) D (d) B

2. Which one of the following is correct route for passage of sperms?
   (a) Testes – Scrotum – Vas deferens – Urethra – Penis
   (b) Scrotum – Testes – Urethra – Vas deferens – Penis
   (c) Testes – Vas deferens – Urethra – Seminal vesicles
   (d) Testes – Vas deferens – Urethra – Penis

3. The newborn baby will be a male or female depends upon the type of the combination of sex chromosomes. The type of sex chromosomes present in humans are X and Y.

   Which of the following combination given below will give birth to P (male)...... and Q (female)......... .
   (a) $P-XY, Q-XX$ (b) $P-Y, Q-X$
   (c) $P-XX, Q-XY$ (d) $P-X, Q-Y$

4. Given below is the information about the type of reproduction taking place in animal X.
   I. Female organism lays hundreds of eggs in water.
   II. Male partner deposits sperm over eggs.
   III. Fertilisation takes place in water.
      Animal X can most likely be
   Codes
   (a) Starfish
   (b) Crocodile
   (c) Hens
   (d) Ostrich

5. Study the table shown below.

	In human
Female reproductive cell	X
Male reproductive cell	Y
Type of fertilisation	Internal
Post-fertilisation structure	Z

   X, Y and Z are correctly identified as

	X	Y	Z
(a)	Ovule	Sperm	Embryo
(b)	Stigma	Pollen	Endosperm
(c)	Ova	Sperm	Zygote
(d)	Sperm	Ova	Zygote

6. Read the statements given below made by three children about reproduction.

I. **Joan** All living beings need an egg and a sperm to reproduce.

II. **Kate** Reproduction is way to prevent the extinction of a species.

III. **Belle** To ensure a higher chance of survival, all living things produce more than one offspring at a time.

Who made a correct statements?
(a) Kate only
(b) Joan and Kate
(c) Belle only
(d) Joan, Kate and Belle

7. Read the statements given below carefully. Identify the statements which are true and choose the correct option.
(a) The process of change by which a larva is transformed into an adult is called metamorphosis.
(b) The young ones look similar to the parents in animals that undergo metamorphosis.
(c) The stages in life cycle of a silkworm are egg → pupa → caterpillar → adult.
(d) A tadpole is adapted to live on land whereas a frog can live in water as well as on land.

8. Look at the given figure carefully. Identify the organism and the mode of reproduction taking place in it.

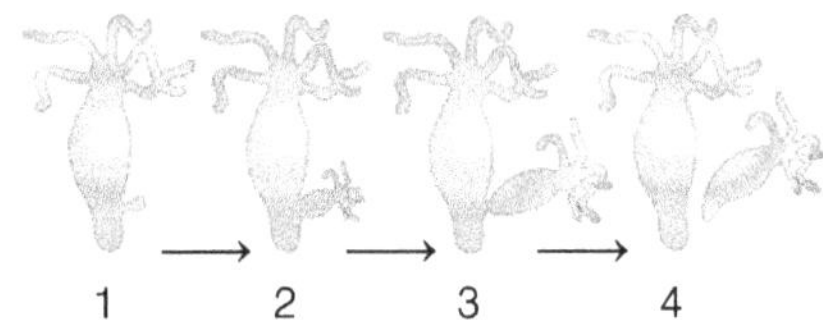

(a) *Planaria*, regeneration
(b) *Hydra*, budding
(c) *Octopus*, regeneration
(d) Yeast, budding

9. The figures given below represent various processes associated with reproduction.

Asexual reproduction is represented by

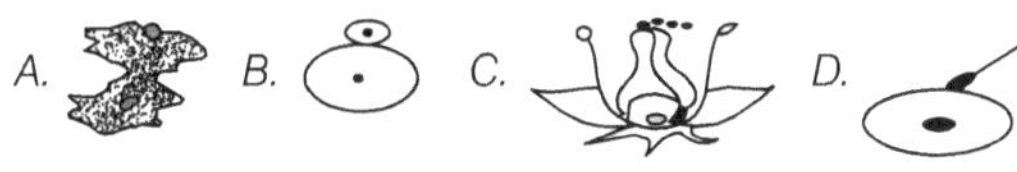

(a) Only *A*   (b) Only *B*
(c) *A* and *B*   (d) *B* and *D*

10. The figure below shows asexual reproduction in *Amoeba*. Identify the step in which cytokinesis occurs.

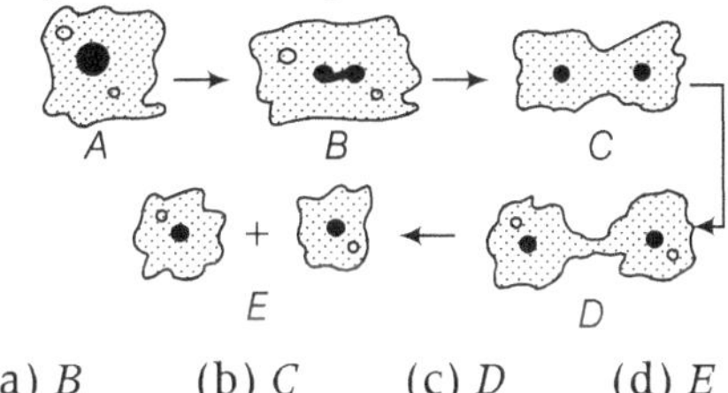

(a) *B*   (b) *C*   (c) *D*   (d) *E*

11. Consider the figures shown below which highlight the part that develops into a new organism by asexual reproduction. An exception to this is

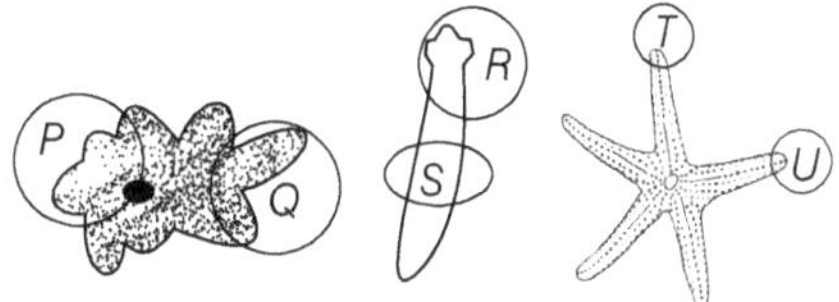

(a) *P, Q, T* and *U*   (b) *R, S, T* and *U*
(c) *Q, R, S* and *T*   (d) *R, T* and *Q*

12. **Assertion** (A) Cloning helps in preserving desirable features of the parent animal for future generation.

Reason (R) Cloning is an asexual method of reproduction.

Which of the following statement is correct?
(a) Both A and R are true and R is the correct explanation of A
(b) Both A and R true, but R is not the correct explanation of A
(c) A is true, but R is false
(d) A is false, but R is true

2 Marks Questions

13. An animal who is known to exhibit-viviparity will show which of the following features.

I. They lay eggs.

II. Eggs are fertilised and developed outside the mother's body always.

III. The sperm meets the ovum inside the mother's body.

IV. All embryos are developed inside the mother's body.

Codes

(a) I, III and IV   (b) I and IV

(c) III and IV   (d) All of these

14. Which of the following statement(s) is/are incorrect?

I. Human females are oviparous as we given birth to young ones.

II. Usually one egg is fertilised by many sperms.

III. The human embryo develops inside the womb of the mother.

IV. After 9 months of development in the mother's ovary, the baby is ready for delivery.

(a) Only II   (b) Both I and III

(c) Both II and III   (d) I, II and IV

15. Read the statements given below.

I. IVF is a treatment for infertility when a woman is able to produce ovum however, problems of the Fallopian tube make fertilisation difficult.

II. The animals that give birth to eggs are known as viviparous animals.

III. Unicellular organisms reproducing by binary fission are referred to as 'immortals because actual death of the parent does not occur.

IV. Snakes always exhibit external fertilisation.

Which of the given statements are incorrect?

(a) II, III and IV   (b) II and IV

(c) I, II, III and IV   (d) I and III

16. Consider the given statements and opt the option correctly defining the statement as either true (T) or false (F).

I. Fertilisation is necessary event in asexual reproduction.

II. The new organism produced by asexual reproduction is clone of its parent.

III. An organism, reproducing through sexual reproduction is known as clone.

IV. *Paramecium* is an unicellular organism which reproduce through multiple fission.

V. Animal cloning is done by the transfer of nucleus from a cell to an enucleated cell.

Codes

	I	II	III	IV	V
(a)	T	F	F	F	T
(b)	T	T	F	T	T
(c)	F	T	F	T	T
(d)	F	F	F	T	T

Age of Adolescence

1 Mark Questions

1. Adam's apple is a protrusion of the 'N' region during the puberty especially marked in the boys. What is N?
   (a) Muscles   (b) Pharynx
   (c) Larynx   (d) Sebaceous gland

2. Given below are characteristics of a hormone secreted when one reaches puberty.
   - It is responsible for breast development.
   - It is secreted in girls.

   The hormone is
   (a) testosterone
   (b) oestrogen
   (c) growth hormone
   (d) Both (a) and (b)

3. Which of the given below options are common in both male and female at puberty?
   A. Pubic hair
   B. Beard
   C. Adam's apple
   D. Deep voice
   E. Broadening of pelvis
   F. Hair under armpits
   (a) A, B, D, E, F   (b) A, C, E, F
   (c) A, F   (d) Only F

4. Select the option that defines the correct age at which the rapid growth occurs in male and female

	Male	Female
(a)	12-14 years	10-13 years
(b)	0-3 years	0-12 years
(c)	10-14 years	14 years onwards
(d)	4-12 years	14 years onwards

5. Read the statements given below.
   I. The first menstrual flow begins at the puberty.
   II. At 45-50 years of age, the menstrual cycle stops.

   Which of the following option correctly highlights the terms that describes the events in I and II?
   (a) Menopause and menstruation, respectively
   (b) Menarche and menstruation, respectively
   (c) Menopause and menarche, respectively
   (d) Menarche and menopause, respectively

6. Which of the following changes take place during puberty?
   A. Milk teeth begin to fall.
   B. Children grow taller rapidly.

C. Breasts begin to developed in females.

D. Voice breaks and begins to deepen in males.

E. Hair begins to grow longer.

(a) A, B and C   (b) B, C and D

(c) A, B, C and D   (d) A, B, C, D and E

7. Adolescent individuals should be cautious about their diet, because

I. Proper diet helps in rapid growth of the body.

II. Eating unmonitored diet since adolescents feel hungry all the time results in obesity.

Select the correct option.

(a) I is correct   (b) II is correct

(c) Both are correct   (d) None are correct

8. A doctor has advised an individual to take regular injection of insulin because of his

(a) high blood pressure

(b) low heat rate

(c) high blood sugar

(d) low metabolic rate

9. *A* is essential for normal functioning of thyroxine hormone secreted by thyroid gland. *A* is identified by which option?

(a) Calcium   (b) Sodium

(c) Magnesium   (d) Iodine

10. Pick the odd one out.

(a) Calcitonin   (b) Testosterone

(c) Adrenaline   (d) Trypsin

11. When adrenaline is secreted in large amount, it prepares our body for action. Identify the changes that will not take place in body with the release of this hormone.

(a) Increased heartbeat

(b) Glucose is secreted in urine

(c) Low blood pressure

(d) Rapid breakdown of carbohydrates (glucose)

12. In the figure given below,

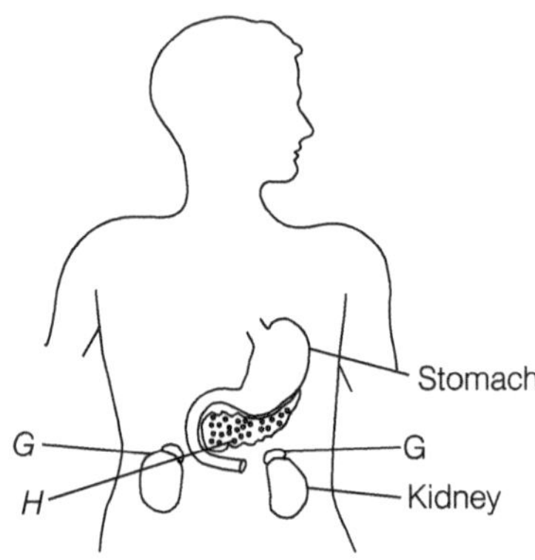

Identify the parts which have following effects on the body.

	effect on the body
I	The overall effect is to prepare the body for emergency situations 'fight or flight'. e.g., running, shouting, etc.
II	Controls the conversion of excess glucose to glycogen in the liver.

Codes

(a) I—*H*   (b) I—*G* and II-*H*

(c) I and II—*G*   (d) I and II—*H*

13. Refer to the figure given below where a woman is exhibiting symptoms of a hormone deficiency.

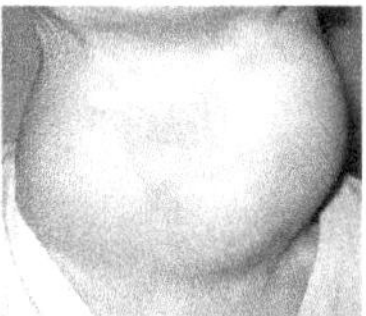

Select the correct statement with respect to the figure.

(a) This condition is associated with a malfunctioning pituitary gland

(b) An insulin injection can temporarily relieve the symptoms of the hormone deficiency

(c) Due to deficiency of thyroxine hormone, causing the gland in neck to enlarge

(d) This occur due to malfunctioning of adrenal gland

2 Marks Questions

14. Gland (X) is located just below the brain and secretes a growth hormone which regulates the development of bones and muscles in the body of an individual. An abnormal secretion, i.e. less (Y) or more (Z) can result in drastic change in the body.

Select the option which correctly identifies X, Y and Z.

	X	Y	Z
(a)	Pituitary	Extremely small body, i.e. Dwarfism	Extremely tall body, i.e. Gigantism
(b)	Hypothalamus	Affects voluntary actions in body	Affects involuntary activities in body
(c)	Thyroid	Weakened body	Strong body
(d)	Adrenal	Heart rate is abnormally slow	Heart rate is abnormally high

15. Study the flow chart given below.

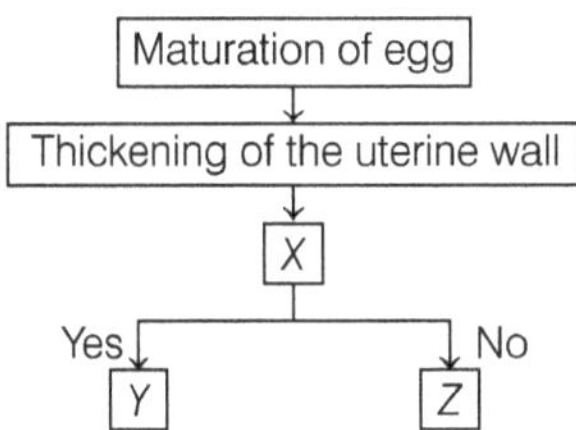

Read the statements given below and select the option which correctly relates with X, Y and Z.

(a) X could be the process of fertilisation where one of the male gametes entering the female reproductive tract fuses with the egg.

(b) For Y-in absence of fertilisation, uterine lining sheds off as menstrual bleeding.

(c) Z-represents establishment of a pregnancy after fusion of gametes.

(d) X-release of eggs from ovaries, Y-fertilisation of gametes and Z-menstruation

16. Read the specification provided below.

I. A acts as an endocrine gland only.

II. B acts as an exocrine gland only.

III. C acts as both the endocrine and exocrine glands.

Identify the glands which can be correctly associated with I, II and III from the box below

(i) Sweat gland, (ii) Pancreas, (iii) Prostrate gland, (iv) Pituitary, (v) Salivary gland, (vi) Adrenal gland, (vii) Liver, (viii) Thymus

	I	II	III
(a)	iv, vi and viii	i, iii and v	ii and vii
(b)	i, iii and v	ii and vii	iv, vi and viii
(c)	ii, vi, vii	i, iii and v	iv and viii
(d)	i, iii, v and vii	ii, iv and vi	viii

17. The figure given below shows the female reproductive tract.

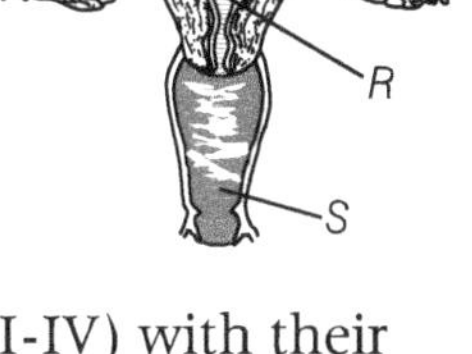

Correlate the given features of the female reproductive tract (I-IV) with their respective parts (P-S).

I. Site of fertilisation.

II. Passage for entry of sperms.

III. Site of gamete production.

IV. Part where development of embryo takes place.

Codes

	I	II	III	IV		I	II	III	IV
(a)	Q	S	P	R	(b)	S	P	R	Q
(c)	P	Q	R	S	(d)	R	S	Q	P

Force and Pressure

1 Mark Questions

1. Which of the following statement(s) about force is/are false?
   A. A force is a push or a pull.
   B. A force can stop a moving object.
   C. A force can change the direction of a moving object.
   D. A force cannot change the speed of a moving object.
   Codes
   (a) A and C (b) Only C
   (c) B and C (d) Only D

2. A box was pushed over an equal distance on four different surfaces. The force needed for each surface was recorded on the table below:

Surface	A	B	C	D
Force needed	400	575	475	375

   On which surface, was the friction least?
   (a) A (b) B (c) C (d) D

3. When the circuit shown in the figure is completed, the hammer strikes the gong.

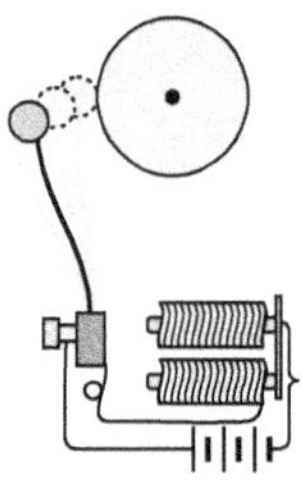

   Which of the following force is responsible for the movement of hammer?
   (a) Gravitational force
   (b) Magnetic force
   (c) Electrostatic force
   (d) Frictional force

4. The diagram given below shows a rubber tyre.

   There are deep treads on the tyre because they _______ .
   (a) increase the stopping distance of the car
   (b) reduce the amount of material used
   (c) enable the tyre to move smoothly
   (d) increase friction

5. Study the diagrams given below:

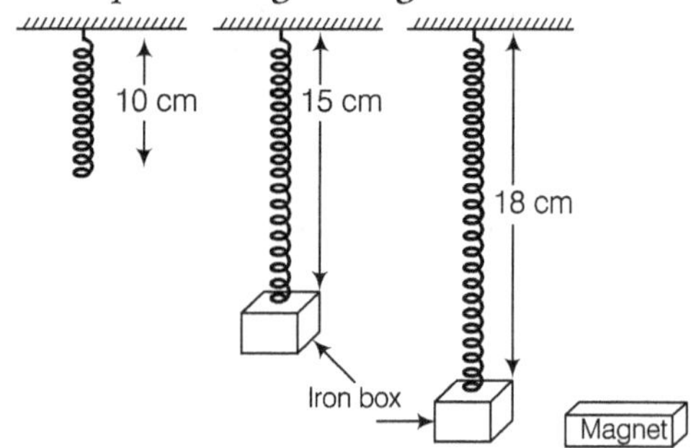

Which type of forces cause the spring to extend in the diagram above?

A. Elastic force exerted by the spring.

B. Magnetic force acting on the iron box.

C. Gravitational force acting on the iron box.

D. Frictional force acting between the iron box and the magnet.

Codes

(a) Only *B*
(b) *B* and *C*
(c) *A, B* and *C*
(d) *A, C* and *D*

6. Which are the correct metric units for friction and weight?

Units		
	Friction	**Weight**
(a)	Newton	Kilogram
(b)	Gram-force	Newton
(c)	Newton	Newton
(d)	Joule	Kilogram

7. We need friction for walking. To put a foot forward, we push the other foot backwards on the ground. The friction between our shoe and the ground acts in the opposite direction and prevents our foot from slipping. Thus, we are able to walk.

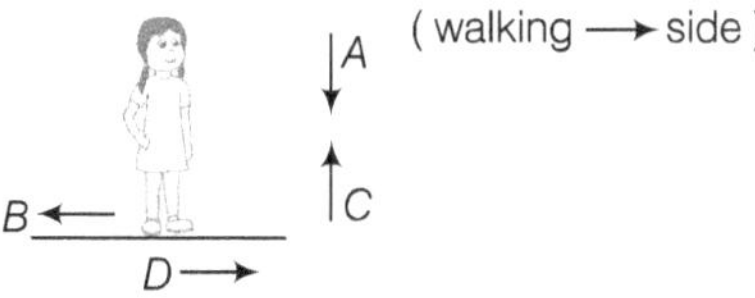

In the above diagram, which arrow represents friction acting between the shoe and the ground?

(a) *A*   (b) *B*   (c) *C*   (d) *D*

8. The figure shows a woman sitting on a chair. The springs in the chair are similar to one another.

Which of the following springs (*A, B, C* or *D*) has the greatest force acting on it?

(a) *A*
(b) *B*
(c) *C*
(d) *D*

9. The effect of force depends on

A. magnitude of the force applied.

B. area over which force is applied.

C. the direction in which force is applied.

D. All of the above

Codes

(a) *A* and *C*
(b) *B* and *C*
(c) Only *D*
(d) *A* and *B*

10. The diagram shows an object hanging from a string. Which of the following is the correct statement about the diagram?

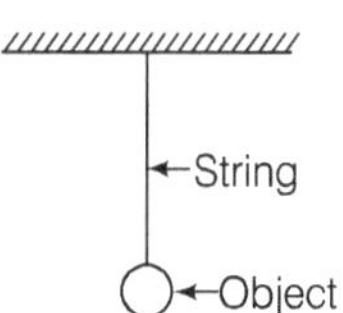

(a) The object does not fall because there is no gravity

(b) The object does not fall because there is friction between the object and the string

(c) The object does not fall because a magnetic force is acting on it

(d) The object does not fall because the string is exerting a force against the Earth's gravity

11. The diagrams below show some ordinary actions. A force is required to carry out each action.

Indicate which of the following is/are correctly matched?

	Action	Force
I.		Pull
II.		Both push and pull
III.		Push
IV.		Push

Codes
(a) Only II   (b) II and III
(c) I and IV   (d) III and IV

12. Porters place a round piece of cloth on their heads when they have to carry heavy bags, so that
(a) the bag does not hurt them
(b) it is easier to balance the bags on their heads
(c) the area of contact of the load with their head increases and the pressure decreases
(d) None of the above

13. Which would be least likely to sink into soft ground?
(a) A loaded lorry with four wheels
(b) A loaded lorry with six wheels
(c) An empty lorry with four wheels
(d) An empty lorry with six wheels

14. A water tank has four taps fixed at points A, B, C, D as shown in the figure given below. The water will flow out at the same pressure from taps at

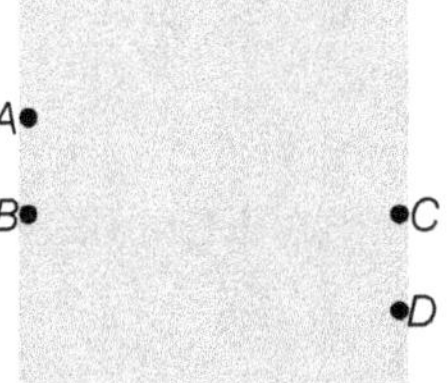

(a) B and C (b) C and D
(c) A and B (d) A and C

15.

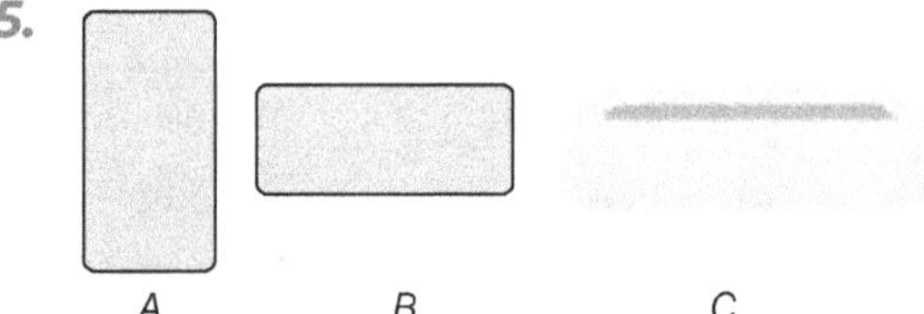

A brick is kept in three different ways on a table as shown in figure. The pressure exerted by the brick on the table will be
(a) maximum in position A
(b) maximum in position B
(c) maximum in position C
(d) equal in all cases

16. Harry says, water exerts pressure on the bottom of the bucket, but Robert says water exerts pressure on the wall of the bucket. Whose statement is correct?
(a) Harry   (b) Robert
(c) Both (a) and (b)   (d) None of these

17. When we inflate the balloons with air, we find that its size increases. The large number of gas molecules collide with each other and create a large
(a) force   (b) pressure
(c) increase in size   (d) increase in mass

18. The diagram below shows the vertical sections of a set of vessels, each containing water up to the same height.

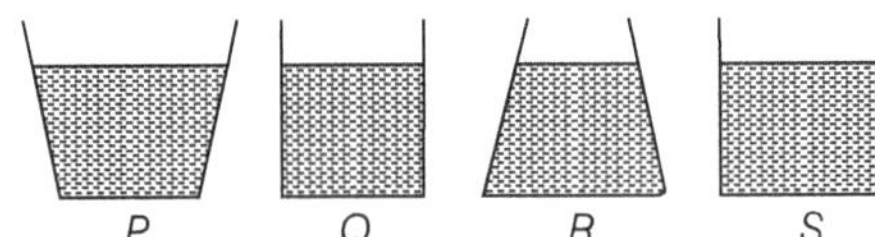

Which of the following statements is correct?

(a) The water exerts the greatest pressure on the base of vessel P.

(b) The water exerts greatest pressure on the base of vessel S.

(c) The water exerts the same force on the base of each vessel.

(d) The water exerts the same pressure on the base of each vessel.

19. Figure below shows a container filled with water. Which of the following statement is correct about pressure of water?

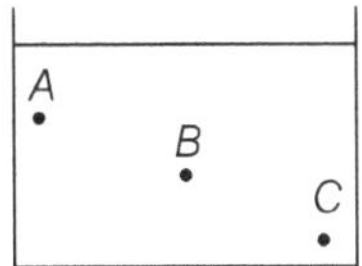

(a) Pressure at $A >$ Pressure at $B >$ Pressure at C

(b) Pressure at $A =$ Pressure at $B =$ Pressure at C

(c) Pressure at $A <$ Pressure at $B >$ Pressure at C

(d) Pressure at $A <$ Pressure at $B <$ Pressure at C

20. A brick of weight 80 N stands upright on the ground as shown. What is the pressure, it exerts on the ground?

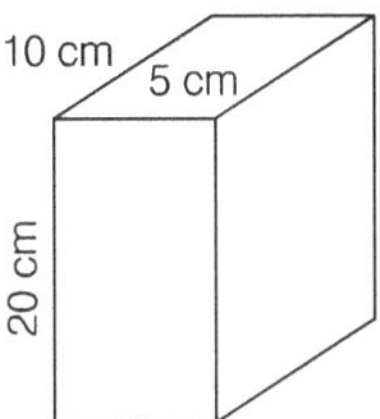

(a) $\dfrac{80}{20 \times 10}$ N/cm^2 (b) $\dfrac{20 \times 10}{80}$ N/cm^2

(c) $\dfrac{80}{10 \times 5}$ N/cm^2 (d) $\dfrac{10 \times 5}{80}$ N/cm^2

21. A container containing water is closed from the top using a frictionless piston. When pressure is applied through the piston, it is transmitted to

(a) the side faces of the container only

(b) bottom of the container only

(c) all the directions

(d) pressure is not at all transmitted

2 Marks Questions

22. When Aryan placed a magnet at the top of the ramp as shown in the figure, the paper clip moved up the ramp and attached to the magnet.

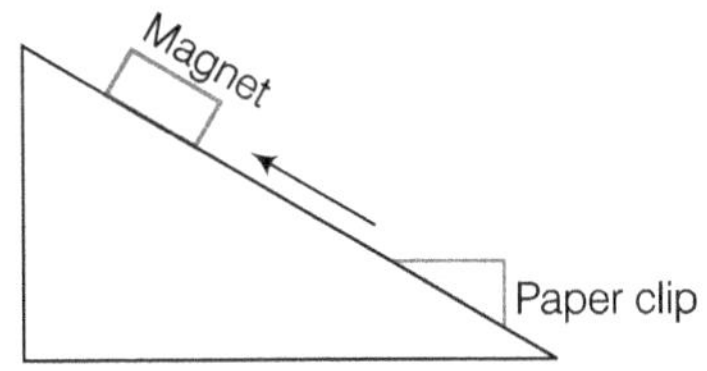

What are the forces acting on the paper clip as it moves along the ramp?

A. Frictional force

B. Magnetic force

C. Elastic potential force

D. Gravitational force

Codes

(a) Only B (b) Both A and D

(c) A, B and D (d) A, B, C and D

23. The pictures show some effects of a force.

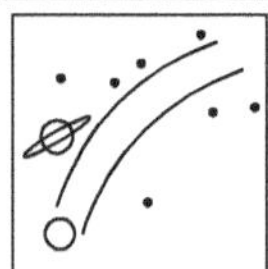  

I. A meteor glowing as it falls through the earth's atmosphere	II. A parachutist falling through the air	III. Brakes slowing down a bicycle

What is the common factor which is acting in these three situations above?

(a) Friction
(b) Gravitational force
(c) Weight
(d) Magnetic force

24. Match the following columns.

	Column I		Column II
A.	A child running to catch the school bus.	1.	Force can make a stationary object to move.
B.	A man blowing a balloon.	2.	Force can stop a moving object.
C.	A woman pushing a table.	3.	Force can change the shape of an object.
D.	A cricketer catching a ball.	4.	Force can make an object move faster.

Codes

	A	B	C	D
(a)	4	3	1	2
(b)	3	2	1	4
(c)	1	2	3	4
(d)	2	4	1	3

25. Tom squeezed four identical tubes of toothpaste from the same height above four different plates as shown below. The initial amount of toothpaste in each tube was same.

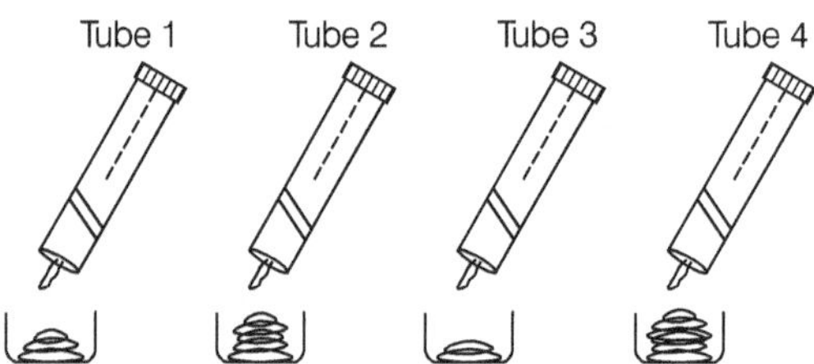

A. More gravity is acted on tube 4 as compared to tube 1.
B. More force was applied on tube 1 as compared to tube 3.
C. There was more toothpaste left in tube 3 compared to tube 2.

Codes
(a) *A* and *B*
(b) *B* and *C*
(c) *A* and *C*
(d) *A, B* and *C*

26. Which of the following statement(s) is/are incorrect?

A. The standard unit of pressure is pascal or Pa.
B. Pressure is area divided by force applied.
C. The bigger the area on which force is applied, the lesser its effect.
D. The knife penetrates easily as the sharp edge has a very small area of contact.

Codes
(a) *A* and *B*
(b) Only *B*
(c) *B* and *C*
(d) *A* and *D*

Friction

1 Mark Questions

1. A man pushes a box across the floor. It slides smoothly but comes to a halt after a while. Which of the given reasons explains why this happen?
   (a) Gravity is acting on the box in the direction opposite to the box's movement.
   (b) Friction is acting on the box in the same direction of the box's movement.
   (c) Friction is acting on the box in the opposite direction of the box's movement.
   (d) The heat produced by the box's movement slows down the movement.

2. Which arrow shows the direction of the force of friction acting on the runner's shoe?

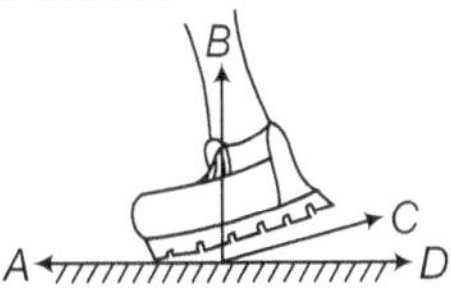

   (a) A   (b) B   (c) C   (d) D

3. An object of weight w is pulled along a rough, horizontal surface by a force P. The force of friction is F.
   Which diagram correctly shows the direction of these forces on the object?

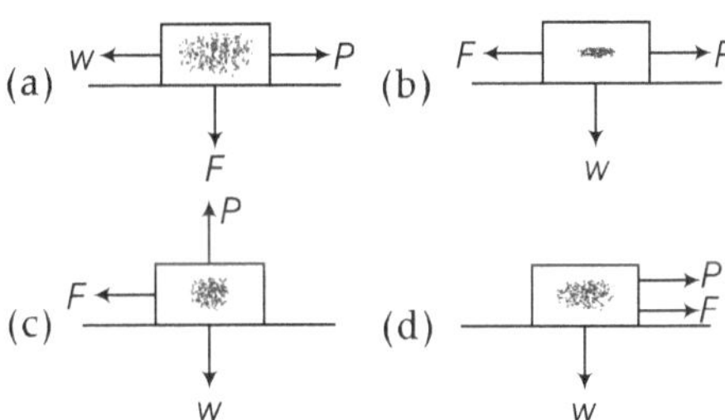

4. Arun carried out an experiment to find out how different surfaces (P, Q, R, S) affect the distance of a car travelling at 60 km/h, which needed to stop once the brakes are applied.

Types of road surface	P	Q	R	S
Stopping distance (m)	20	17	18	15

   Which type of road will provide the most friction for the car to stop?
   (a) P (b) R
   (c) S (d) Q

5. In a large commercial complex, there are four ways to reach the main road. One of the paths has loose soil, the second is laid with polished marble, the third is laid with bricks and the fourth has gravel surface. It is raining heavily and Paheli wishes to reach

the main road. The path on which she is least likely to slip is

(a) loose soil   (b) polished marble
(c) bricks   (d) gravel

6. Whenever the surfaces in contact tend to move or move with respect to each other, the force of friction comes into play

(a) only if the objects are solid
(b) only if one of the two objects is liquid
(c) only if one of the two objects is gaseous
(d) irrespective of whether the objects are solid, liquid or gaseous

7. In the figure given below, a boy is shown pushing the box from right to left.

The force of friction will act on the box

(a) from right to left ($\leftarrow$)
(b) from left to right ($\rightarrow$)
(c) vertically downwards ($\downarrow$)
(d) vertically upwards ($\uparrow$)

8. Ram pushes the box by applying a force of 500 N in horizontal direction, so that the box slides on the floor as shown in figure. Find the point, where the frictional force acting on the box is maximum.

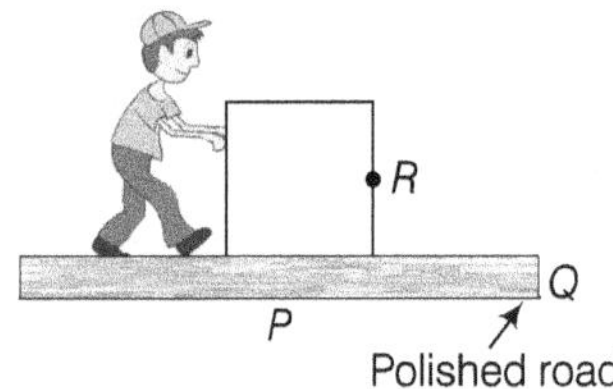

(a) P (b) Q
(c) R (d) P, Q and R

9. When friction is acting in the direction of P, then in which direction do you think the force is applied?

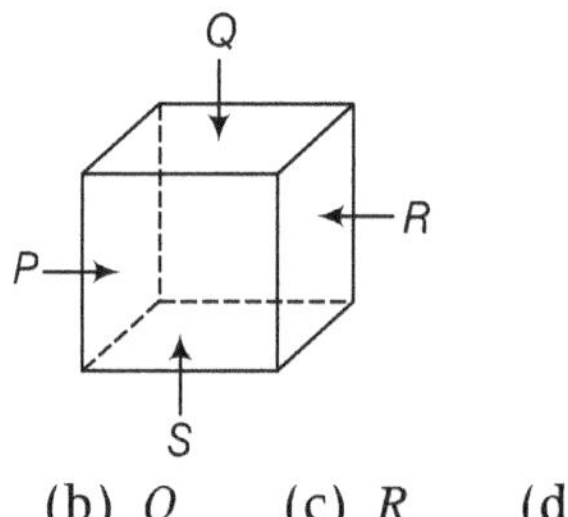

(a) P (b) Q (c) R (d) S

10. Alida runs her toy car on dry marble floor, wet marble floor, newspaper and towel spread on the floor. The force of friction acting on the car on different surfaces in increasing order will be

(a) wet marble floor, dry marble floor, newspaper and towel
(b) newspaper, towel, dry marble floor, wet marble floor
(c) towel, newspaper, dry marble floor, wet marble floor
(d) wet marble floor, dry marble floor, towel, newspaper

11. The diagram given below shows a ball rolling down a slope. The ball comes to a stop by itself. Which of the following statements describes the most likely caused of the ball to stop?

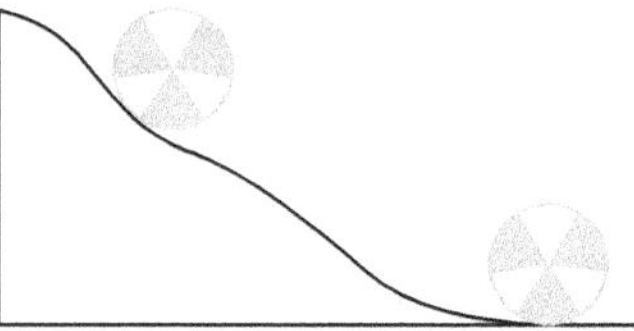

(a) The heat produced as a result of its motion
(b) The speed produced as a result of its motion
(c) The friction between the ball and the surface
(d) The energy produced as a result of its motion

12. A person throws four stones having the same weight on four different surfaces as icy, dry, sandy and cemented. If same force is applied in throwing, then on which surface the stone will cover maximum distance?
(a) Icy surface   (b) Dry surface
(c) Sandy surface   (d) Cemented surface

13. Door hinge is a jointed device that allows the turning of a door. If we apply oil on door hinges, the friction will
(a) increase
(b) decrease
(c) disappear altogether
(d) will remain unchanged

14. A boy rolls a rubber ball on a wooden surface. The ball travels a short distance before coming to rest. To make the same ball travel longer distance before coming to rest, he may
(a) spread a carpet on the wooden surface
(b) cover the ball with a piece of cloth
(c) sprinkle talcum powder on the wooden surface
(d) sprinkle sand on the wooden surface

15. Four children were asked to arrange forces due to rolling, static and sliding frictions in a decreasing order. Their arrangements are given below. Choose the correct arrangements.
(a) Rolling, static, sliding
(b) Rolling, sliding, static
(c) Static, sliding, rolling
(d) Sliding, static, rolling

16. You must have observed a bull ploughing the field. A bull struggles in its first few steps to pull a plough. Why is it so?

(a) Static friction is greater than sliding friction
(b) Sliding friction is greater than rolling friction
(c) No frictional force acts after the cart is in motion
(d) Air friction is greater during the first few steps of motion

17. A rocket and a bird have a streamlined shaped body (as shown in figure below) because

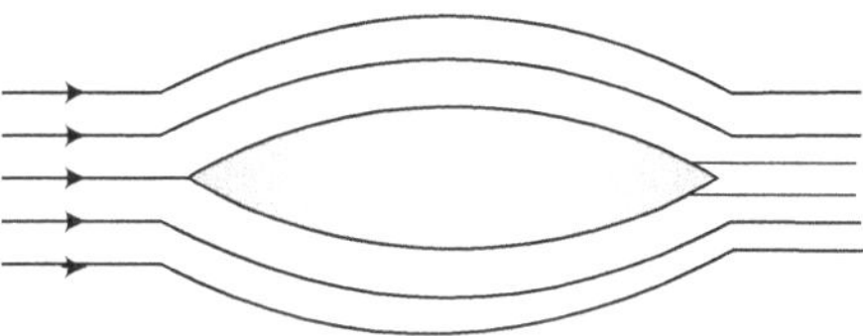

Streamlined body

(a) it gives force to move
(b) it moves through air with minimum friction
(c) it increases the speed of the object
(d) All of the above

18. The bottle in the picture is rolling from *P* towards *S*. From which direction should frictional force act to slow down the rolling bottle?

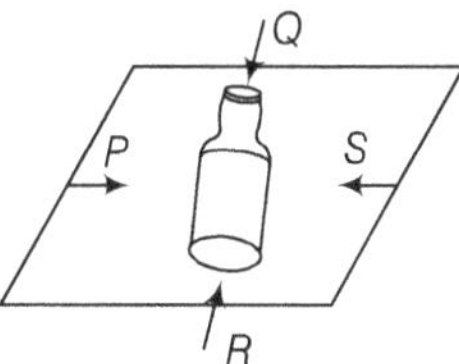

(a) *P*   (b) *Q*
(c) *S*   (d) *R*

19. Roller-skating is the travelling on surfaces with roller-skates. It is a form of sport and can also be a form of transportation.
Why do we move faster on roller-skates than on shoes?

(a) The roller-skates have rollers to reduce friction.

(b) The roller-skates have more surface in contact with ground.

(c) The roller-skates have no gravitational force.

(d) The roller-skates absorb heat from the ground.

20. We need energy to overcome friction. During friction, unwanted heat energy is produced. Friction can be reduced by the use of which of the following?

   I. Rollers   II. Gears

 III. Lubricants   IV. Ball bearings

Codes

(a) I, II and III   (b) I, III and IV

(c) II, III and IV   (d) I, II and IV

21. When we apply some force on an object held stationary at a place, then force of friction comes into play in direction opposite to the direction of motion of the object.

When the applied force is doubled (object is still at rest), then friction becomes

(a) doubled   (b) halved

(c) quadrupled   (d) zero

22. Given below is a list of some items/quantities.

   I. Lubricants   II. Streamlined bodies

 III. Heat   IV. Polished surface

   V. Ball bearing

Pick the odd one(s) out from the above list.

(a) I and IV   (b) II and IV

(c) Only III   (d) III and V

23. Select the incorrect statement.

(a) Grass and dampness on a cricket ground increase friction.

(b) Friction causes parts of a machine to wear out.

(c) Moving parts of a car (e.g. wheel) become hot due to friction.

(d) Friction is less on a dry floor than a wet floor.

24. If the static friction between two surfaces X and Y is found to be 20 N, then the rolling friction between these two surfaces would be

(a) 25 N (b) 50 N (c) 20 N (d) 5 N

2 Marks Questions

25. Which of the following statement(s) related to friction is/are correct?

Friction acts

   I. only when an object is in motion.

  II. whether an object is moving or not.

 III. on a stationary object only.

 IV. on an object opposite to the direction of its motion.

Codes

(a) I and IV   (b) II and IV

(c) Only III   (d) Only II

26. **Statement I** If friction is not present in nature, then life will be easy.

Statement II Without friction, there would be no reaction from ground in a forward direction.

(a) Only statement I is correct.

(b) Only statement II is correct.

(c) Both statements are correct.

(d) Both statements are incorrect.

27. State [T] for True and [F] for False.

   I. Friction occurs because most surfaces are not rough.

II. The force of friction is dependent on the weight of body.

III. If an object starts moving, it would never stop if there were no friction.

IV. Friction produces motion.

Codes

	I	II	III	IV
(a)	T	T	F	T
(b)	F	F	T	F
(c)	F	T	T	F
(d)	T	F	F	T

28. Which one of following statement(s) given below is/are correct?

    I. The force of friction depends on the area of the surfaces in contact.

    II. Motion opposes friction.

    III. It is not possible to cut wood without friction between the saw and wood.

    IV. Solids and liquids do not allow things to move in or over them.

    Codes
    (a) Only I   (b) Only II
    (c) Only III   (d) Only IV

29. Which of the following statement(s) given below is/are incorrect?

    I. Friction is useful to us in many ways.

II. Meteoroids entering the Earth's atmosphere are burnt up by heat generated from friction with the water.

III. We cannot walk without friction between our feet and the ground.

IV. Rolling friction is greater than static friction.

Codes
(a) I, II and III   (b) Only II
(c) I, II and IV   (d) II and IV

30. Match the following columns.

	Column I		Column II
A.	Rough surface	1.	No friction
B.	Wheels	2.	More friction
C.	Streamlined bodies	3.	Less friction
D.	Space	4.	Submarines and rockets

Codes

	A	B	C	D
(a)	2	3	4	1
(b)	1	2	4	3
(c)	3	1	2	4
(d)	2	3	1	4

13

Sound

1 Mark Questions

1. When a whistle is blown, it produces sound. Which part of whistle vibrates to produce sound?
   (a) Body of whistle
   (b) Mouth of the person
   (c) Air
   (d) All of the above

2. Naveen arranged seven similar glasses with water on the table. Each glass had different levels of water. He played different tunes on it using two sticks to tap the water filled glasses. What has he made?

   (a) Harmonica   (b) Sarangi
   (c) Jal tarang   (d) Ghatak

3. A student performs the following activity as shown in the figure below:

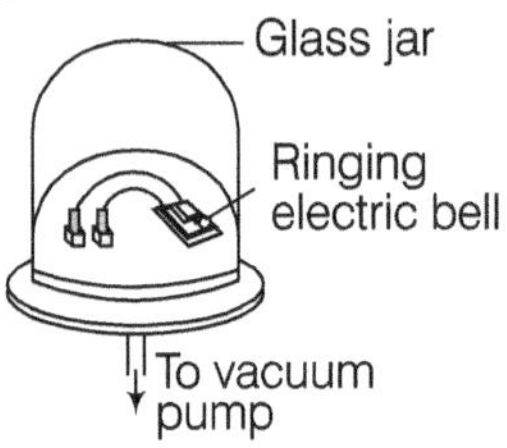

   What do you think happened as air was pumped out of the jar and he rang the bell?
   (a) The sound became louder
   (b) The sound became fainter first and louder once all the air was pumped out
   (c) The sound could not be heard anymore
   (d) The sound was the same as before

4. A list of medium is given as below:
   I. Wood
   II. Water
   III. Air
   IV. Vacuum

   In which of these media can sound travel?
   (a) I and II   (b) I, II and III
   (c) III and IV   (d) II, III and IV

5. Take four jars with different amount of water. Hit the rim of the jars with the pencil. In which one of the following cases, the intensity of sound will be maximum?
   (a) The jar filled completely
   (b) Jar half filled
   (c) Jar filled less than half
   (d) Jar filled more than half

6. Which of the following does not produce a sound wave?

    I. A bell ringing in a glass jar with all the air pumped out.

    II. A gun fired in a room with no echoes.

    IV. A hammer hitting a block of rubber.

    V. An explosion in outer space.

    Codes
    (a) I, II and III   (b) II, III and IV
    (c) Only IV   (d) I and IV

7. What is the correct order(slowest $\rightarrow$ fastest) for the speed of sound in air, steel and water?

    (a) Air, steel, water   (b) Air, water, steel
    (c) Water, air, steel   (d) Water, steel, air

8. A person tries to hear an approaching train by pressing his ear on the track. He will be able to hear because

    (a) sound travels faster in solids
    (b) sound travels faster in air
    (c) railway track starts vibrating
    (d) None of the above

9. The names of musical instruments are given as below:

    I. Guitar   II. Sitar   III. Tabla

    IV. Violin   V. Piano

    Pick the odd ones out from the above instruments.

    (a) I and II   (b) III and IV
    (c) III and V   (d) IV and V

10. Which of the following is/are incorrect about the production and propagation of sound?

    I. Sound is produced by vibrations.

    II. Sound requires a medium for propagation.

    III. Light and sound both require a medium for propagation.

    IV. Sound travels slower than light.

    Codes
    (a) I and IV   (b) I, III and IV
    (c) Only III   (d) III and IV

11. Human ear is a very sensitive device that has various parts which performs different functions to transmit sound from surroundings to the brain. Which part of the ear does not vibrate while detecting sound?

    (a) Eardrum   (b) Anvil
    (c) Stirrup   (d) Eustachian tube

12. Which of the following is not a use of ultrasound?

    I. Sonography to check development of unborn babies.

    II. Ultrasound for cleaning tartar from teeth.

    III. Ultrasound for echolocation to determine depth of ocean.

    IV. Ultrasound treatment of tumours in patients suffering from cancer.

    Codes
    (a) I and III   (b) Only II
    (c) Only III   (d) II, III and IV

13. Four different whistles when blown, emit pure notes with the frequencies shown :

    0.1 kHz, 1 kHz, 10 kHz, 100 kHz

    How many of the frequencies are above the normal audible range for humans?

    (a) 1   (b) 2   (c) 3   (d) 4

14. The sound from the surrounding entering into our ear is collected by pinna. The sound which enters into our ear is not of high amplitude. They are amplified inside our ear. The part of the ear which does this work is

    (a) eardrum
    (b) hammer, anvil and stirrup
    (c) ear canal
    (d) cochlea

15. Some animals like elephants, whales and rhinoceroses can produce infrasonic waves. Which of the following is infrasonic sound?
(a) 15 Hz
(b) 150 Hz
(c) 1500 Hz
(d) 15000 Hz

16. Choose a correct option from the following matrix.

	Pitch	Loudness	Noise	Music
(a)	Amplitude	Frequency	Irregular vibration	Regular vibration
(b)	Frequency	Amplitude	Regular vibration	Irregular vibration
(c)	Frequency	Amplitude	Irregular vibration	Regular vibration
(d)	Amplitude	Frequency	Regular vibration	Irregular vibration

17. Sonic vibrations were sent down from a ship return after 20 s. What is the depth of the sea if the speed of sound in water is 1.5 kms^{-1}?
(a) 150 m   (b) 3 km
(c) 15 km   (d) 750 m

18. Bees which are not carrying honey, fly with a flapping frequency of 440 Hz while those which are carrying honey, fly with a flapping frequency of 300 Hz. The sound made by bees which are not carrying honey has
(a) a long pitch
(b) a higher pitch
(c) a smaller loudness
(d) a greater loudness

19. A list of various characteristics of sound is given as below:
  I. Shrillness   II. Pitch
 III. Frequency   IV. Loudness
  V. Speed

Pick the odd ones out from the above characteristics.
(a) I and III   (b) I and IV
(c) IV and V   (d) II and V

20. Lightning can be seen the moment it occurs. Paheli observes lightning in her area. She hears the sound 5 s after she observed lightning. How far is she from the place where lightning occurs?
(speed of sound $= 330$ m/s).
(a) 16.5 km   (b) 1.65 km
(c) 165 km   (d) 3.35 km

21. The sound from a mosquito is produced when it vibrates its wings at an average rate of 500 vibrations/s. What is the time-period of vibration?
(a) 2 s   (b) 0.2 s   (c) 0.02 s (d) 0.002 s

22. A child plays a note on a trumpet. She then plays a louder note of higher pitch. How do the amplitude and frequency of the second sound compare with the first?

	Amplitude of second sound	Frequency of second sound
(a)	Larger	Larger
(b)	Larger	Smaller
(c)	Smaller	Larger
(d)	Smaller	Smaller

2 Marks Questions

23. Find the true (T) and false (F) statements and choose the correct option from codes given below.

   I. A tuning fork, a guitar string and the skin of a drum produce sound because they are in the state of vibration.

  II. Light requires a medium to travel but sound can travel in vacuum.

 III. Sound propagates in parallel directions only.

 IV. The drum and tabla are percussion instruments.

Codes

	I	II	III	IV		I	II	III	IV
(a)	T	F	T	F	(b)	T	T	T	F
(c)	F	T	F	T	(d)	T	F	F	T

24. Which of the following statement(s) is/are correct?

   I. The lower limit of frequency that can be heard by the average human ear is 20 Hz.

  II. Sound higher than 20000 Hz is called infrasonic.

 III. Auditory nerve carries the signals from inner ear to the brain.

 IV. Infrasonic waves are used to measure the depth of a sea.

Codes

(a) Only I (b) I and III
(c) III and IV (d) All of these

25. Which of the following statement(s) is/are incorrect about noise?

   I. Vehicles should have proper silencers.

  II. Sudden exposure to high noise can cause a heart attack.

 III. Use of amplifiers and loudspeakers should not be restricted.

 IV. Planting of trees helps reduce noise.

Codes

(a) I, II and III (b) II and III
(c) Only II (d) I and IV

26. State [T] for True and [F] for False.

   I. Infrasonic waves are used to kill bacteria in liquids.

  II. Ultrasonic waves are produced by the vibration of the Earth's surface during the Earthquake.

 III. Noise pollution may cause partial hearing impairment.

 IV. The sound having frequency less than 20 Hz are called infrasound.

Codes

	I	II	III	IV
(a)	T	T	F	F
(b)	F	T	T	F
(c)	T	F	F	T
(d)	F	F	T	T

27. Match the following columns.

Column I		Column II
A. Oscillation	1.	Maximum displacement of a wave.
B. Amplitude	2.	Distance between two consecutive peaks.
C. Frequency	3.	To and fro motion of wave.
D. Wavelength	4.	Number of oscillations of sound wave.

Codes

	A	B	C	D		A	B	C	D
(a)	3	1	4	2	(b)	3	2	4	1
(c)	4	1	3	3	(d)	4	2	1	3

Chemical Effects of Electric Current

1 Mark Questions

1. When current is passed through molten sodium chloride, then
   (a) sodium is deposited at the positive electrode and chlorine gas is formed at the negative electrode
   (b) sodium is evaporated and chloride ions are formed at the negative electrode
   (c) sodium is deposited at the positive electrode and chlorine is deposited at the negative electrode
   (d) sodium is deposited at the negative electrode and the chlorine is deposited at the positive electrode

2. A box of items is given as below:

   I. Milk   II. Impure water
   III. Honey   IV. Glass

   Which of these conduct electricity?
   (a) I and III   (b) Only II
   (c) II and III   (d) Only IV

3. A scientist needed a liquid conductor for his experiment. He found that he had only pure water. What should he do to make it a conductor?
   (a) Heat it to 100°C
   (b) Add sugar to it
   (c) Add salt to it
   (d) None of the above

4. In an electrochemical cell, the two electrodes connected with battery are dipped into electrolyte. The electrode connected to positive terminal of a battery is
   (a) anode   (b) pole
   (c) cathode   (d) photodiode

5. Which of the following is a device used to determine whether a substance is a good or poor conductor of electricity?
   (a) Electric tester   (b) Conduction tester
   (c) Cathode ray   (d) Spark plug

6. Which of the following statement(s) is/are incorrect?
   A. Conductors have more free charge on the surface than insulators.
   B. Conductors allow charge to flow through them more easily than insulators.
   C. Non-metals are good conductors.
   D. Electric wires are usually covered by insulators.

   Codes
   (a) A and B   (b) B and C
   (c) Only C   (d) Only D

7. An electric current is defined as the flow of charge through a conductor. An electric current can produce
   (a) heating effect
   (b) chemical effect
   (c) magnetic effect
   (d) All of the above

8. When electric current is passed through a conducting solution, there is a change of colour of the solution. This indicates
   (a) the chemical effect of current
   (b) the heating effect of current
   (c) the magnetic effect of current
   (d) the lightning effect of current

9. Like solids, some liquids also conduct electricity. Such liquids are called electrolytes. An electrolyte
   (a) has positive charge
   (b) has negative charge
   (c) should be able to conduct charge without dissociating
   (d) should be able to form positive and negative ions

10. A box of liquids is given as below:
    I. Lemon juice
    II. Sugar solution
    III. Dilute hydrochloric acid
    IV. Distilled water

    Which of the following liquids does not conduct electricity?
    (a) I, II and IV   (b) Only III
    (c) III and IV   (d) II and IV

11. In a metallic wire, the free electrons are responsible for the flow of electric current. When the ends of metallic wire are not connected to a battery, then
    (a) electrons move from positive electrode to negative electrode
    (b) electrons move from negative electrode to positive electrode
    (c) electrons move in random directions
    (d) protons move in random direction in such a way that their net movement in a unit volume is zero

12. Electroplating is one of the main uses of electrolysis. A metal is released in the electrolysis of a salt. It gets deposited on the
    (a) anode
    (b) cathode
    (c) half on anode, half on cathode
    (d) side of the container

13. Which of the following solution will not make the bulb in the diagram glow?

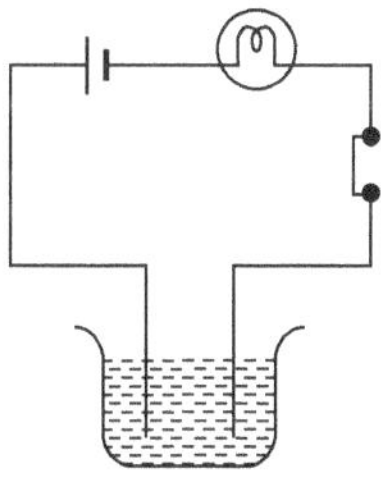

    (a) Sodium chloride
    (b) Copper sulphate
    (c) Silver nitrate
    (d) Sugar solution in diluted water

14. Arun went to the seaside. He collected some seawater for testing. He tested some drinking water and also the seawater with his tester. He finds that his tester needle deflects more in case of seawater. Why?
    (a) Because, drinking water is a poor conductor
    (b) Because, seawater is a poor conductor
    (c) Because, seawater is an insulator
    (d) Because, seawater is very salty and salt solution is a good conductor of electricity

15. In case of a fire, before the fireman uses the water hoses to throw water. To douse fire they shut off the electricity supply of the area. Why?
(a) To prevent electrocution because ordinary water is a conductor of electricity
(b) To ensure electricity is not affected by this disturbance
(c) So that there is a uninterrupted flow of water
(d) None of the above

16. Which of the following may not be an effect when current flows through a conducting solution?
I. Change of colour of solution
II. Bubbles of gases
III. Deposits of metal on electrodes
Codes
(a) Only I
(b) Only II
(c) Only III
(d) None of the above

17. Select the correct statement.
(a) LED consumes much lower. electricity, so they are economical.
(b) They find applications for few purposes.
(c) Ordinary bulb can glow whether the current supply is high or low.
(d) LEDs are available only in yellow colour.

18. A list of metals is given below
I. Silver
II. Gold
III. Sodium
IV. Chromium
V. Aluminium

Pick the odd ones out from the given metals.
(a) I and III
(b) II and IV
(c) III and V
(d) II and V

19. Select the incorrect statement.
(a) We can use a magnetic compass in a circuit of a conduction tester.
(b) We can use a LED in the circuit of a conduction tester.
(c) We can use a torch bulb or LED in the circuit of a conduction tester.
(d) We can use iron filings in the circuit of a conduction tester.

20. Boojho's uncle has set up an electroplating factory near his village. He should dispose off the waste of the factory
(a) in the nearby river
(b) in the nearby pond
(c) in the nearby cornfield
(d) according to the disposal guidelines of the local authority

2 Marks Questions

21. Match the following columns.

	Column I		Column II
A.	CFLs	1.	Cost efficient
B.	LEDs	2.	Non-conducting
C.	Closed path	3.	Contain toxic mercury
D.	Milk	4.	Electric circuit

Codes

	A	B	C	D
(a)	2	1	4	3
(b)	3	1	4	2
(c)	1	2	4	3
(d)	2	1	3	4

22. State (T) for True and (F) for false.

I. Most liquids that are good conductors are solution of acids, bases and salts.

II. All wires used in electric circuits should be covered with conducting material.

III. Magnetic effect of current is responsible for the glow of the bulb in an electric circuit.

IV. Adding common salt to distilled water makes it good conductor.

V. Cathode is positive electrode.

Codes

	I	II	III	IV	V
(a)	F	T	F	T	T
(b)	T	F	F	T	F
(c)	T	T	T	F	F
(d)	F	F	F	T	T

23. Match the following columns.

	Column I		Column II
A.	Insulator	1.	Citric acid
B.	Conductor	2.	Poor Conductor
C.	Electrolyte in lemon juice	3.	Distilled water
D.	Non-metal	4.	Sea water

Codes

	A	B	C	D		A	B	C	D
(a)	4	3	1	2	(b)	4	3	2	1
(c)	3	4	1	2	(d)	3	4	2	1

24. Match the following columns.

	Column I		Column II
A.	Chromium	1.	Food cans
B.	Gold plating	2.	Prevents rusting
C.	Tin	3.	Artificial jewellery
D.	Electroplating	4.	Scratch proof

Codes

	A	B	C	D		A	B	C	D
(a)	2	3	4	1	(b)	4	2	1	3
(c)	4	2	3	1	(d)	4	3	1	2

25. Which of the following statements is/are correct?

I. Electrolyte is more conducting than metal.

II. Ions move slow than electrons.

III. Rain water is a conductor of electricity.

IV. If a little salt is dissolved to the distilled water, it becomes good conductor of electricity.

Codes

(a) I and II   (b) III and IV

(c) I, II and III   (d) II, III and IV

Chapter 15

Some Natural Phenomenon

1 Mark Questions

1. A trident shaped device on top of tall buildings which provide a low resistance path to the ground and protect buildings from effect of lightning, is called
   (a) lightning inductor
   (b) lightning conductor
   (c) lightning generator
   (d) electroscope

2. A thunderstorm is a type of storm characterised by the presence of lightning and thunder. During thunderstorm
   (a) negative charges accumulate near lower edges of cloud
   (b) negative charges accumulate near upper edges of cloud
   (c) negative charges do not accumulate in the cloud
   (d) Both (a) and (b) are true

3. Two charged objects are brought close to each other. Choose the most appropriate statement from the following options.
   (a) They may attract
   (b) They may repel
   (c) They may attract or repel depending on the type of charges they carry
   (d) There will be no effect

4. Lightning usually occurs within a cloud in the sky and is called sheet lightning. Storm clouds carry electric charges.
   Which type of charges are stored in clouds?
   (a) Positive
   (b) Negative
   (c) Neutral
   (d) Both (a) and (b)

5. Aman's mother told him not to carry an umbrella during a thunderstorm. Why did she say so?
   (a) The umbrella will not withstand the storm
   (b) The metal tip of umbrella can attract lightning
   (c) The umbrella may break
   (d) A raincoat is better than an umbrella

6. Pankhul was driving his car when he got caught in a thunderstorm. What do you suggest that he should do to protect himself?
   (a) Get out of the car and take cover under an open shaded area
   (b) Run to the nearest tree
   (c) Stand near an electric pole
   (d) Remain in car

7. Which gas is produced in air during lightning?
   (a) Carbon dioxide (b) Hydrogen
   (c) Ozone   (d) Oxygen

8. When, we remove polyester or woolen cloth in dark, we can see spark and hear a cracking sound. These are due to
   (a) static electricity
   (b) current electricity
   (c) reflection of light
   (d) refraction of light

9. During a thunderstorm, an observer can see lightning before hearing its thunder. Why does he see lightning before he hear thunder?
   (a) Sound travels slower than light.
   (b) Sound needs a medium to travel through.
   (c) Sound cannot reflect off surfaces as easily as light.
   (d) Sound is not processed by the brain as fast as light.

10. Raman said to his son that it is safer to use mobile phones and cordless phones during a thunderstorm. Why did he say so?
    (a) Because, they are not connected to wires which can be affected by lightning
    (b) Because, we can contact people when we are afraid
    (c) As, they are our connect to the outside world
    (d) None of the above

11. Select the correct statement.
    (a) The process of electric discharge between clouds and the earth or between different clouds causes lightning.
    (b) Lightning conductor can protect buildings from the effect of thunder.
    (c) One end of the lightning rod is kept out in the air and the other is kept open on the ground.
    (d) Electrical lights must be put off during a thunderstorm.

12. The instrument that is used to detect an earthquake is
    (a) anemometer
    (b) electroscope
    (c) barometer
    (d) seismograph

13. Tsunami is also a destructive natural phenomenon which can cause a huge loss of life and property (houses and other buildings, etc.) Which of the following is not likely to cause tsunami?
    (a) A major nuclear explosion under sea
    (b) Earthquake
    (c) Volcanic eruption
    (d) Lightning

14. The structure of earth consists of three main layers: core, mantle and crust. The earth's plate responsible for causing earthquake is
    (a) crust   (b) mantle
    (c) inner core   (d) outer core

15. Consider the list of terms given below:
    I. Seismic zone
    II. Fault zone
    III. Mantle
    IV. Inner core

    The boundaries of the Earth's plate are known as
    (a) I and II
    (b) I and III
    (c) III and IV
    (d) II, III and IV

16. Consider the list of terms given below:

   I. Tsunami

  II. Landslide

 III. Floods

 IV. Lightning

Earthquake can cause

(a) I, II and III   (b) II and IV

(c) II, III and IV   (d) III and IV

17. Which of the following statement(s) is/are correct?

   I. The outermost layer of earth is in one piece.

  II. Each fragment of the earth is called a tectonic plate.

 III. Tectonic plates are always at rest.

 IV. The boundaries of the plates are the zones where earthquake occurs.

Codes

(a) I and II   (b) II and IV

(c) I and III   (d) Only IV

18. Consider the different words given as below:

   I. Seismograph

  II. Fault lines

 III. Electrograph

 IV. Richter scale

Pick the odd one out from the above.

(a) I and III   (b) Only II

(c) Only III   (d) I and IV

2 Marks Questions

19. Assertion (A) Tsunamis are a huge catastrophic disaster which can be caused by an earthquake on the sea floor.

Reason (R) An earthquake is caused by the movement of tectonic plates.

(a) Both a and R are true and R is the correct explantion of A.

(b) Both A and R are true, but R is not the correct explanation of A.

(c) A is true, but R is false.

(d) A is false, but R is true.

20. State (T) for True and (F) for False.

   I. Richter scale is a device which tests whether an object is carrying charge or not.

  II. A lightning conductor protects building from the effect of lightning by the process of discharging.

 III. A lightning rod must be taller than the structure it is meant for.

 IV. In an electrical storm, the upper portion of the cloud is negative and the lower portion is positive.

Codes

	I	II	III	IV			I	II	III	IV
(a)	F	F	T	T		(b)	F	F	T	F
(c)	T	F	F	T		(d)	T	T	F	T

21. State (T) for true and (F) for false.

   I. Tides in the ocean cause tsunami.

  II. Tsunami is the huge waves created during earthquake.

 III. Earthquakes can be predicted in advance.

 IV. The plates of the outermost layer of the earth are always in continuous motion.

Codes

	I	II	III	IV			I	II	III	IV
(a)	T	F	T	F		(b)	F	T	F	T
(c)	T	T	F	F		(d)	F	F	T	T

22. Which of these things would you do if you live in the earthquake prone area?

    I. You would keep an emergency kit always ready.
    II. You would have an open book shelves and open cupboards.
    III. You would fix the cupboards to the walls.
    IV. You would not keep breakable items on the upper shelves.

    Codes
    (a) Only III is correct
    (b) Both I and III are correct
    (c) I, III and IV are correct
    (d) All of the above

23. Earthquakes at two places A and B were measured by a seismograph which recorded the magnitude as 2 and 4.

    he magnitude of tremors and the destructive energy at A and B can be compared as
    (a) tremors at B are two times those at place A
    (b) tremors at B are four times those at place A
    (c) tremors at B are 100 times those at place A
    (d) tremors at B are 1000 times those at place A

Light

1 Mark Questions

1. Which of these depict diffused reflection?

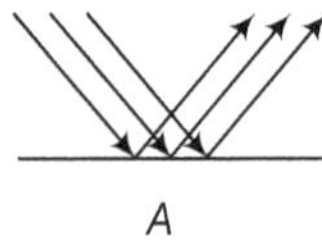

A

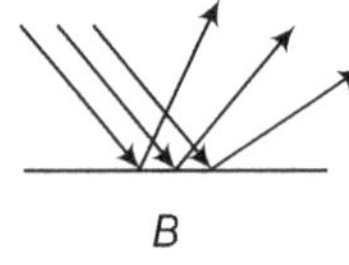

B

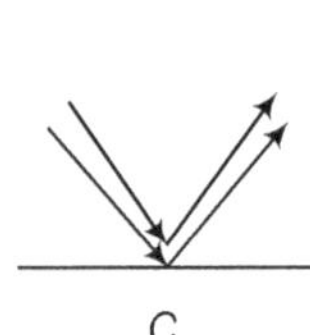

C

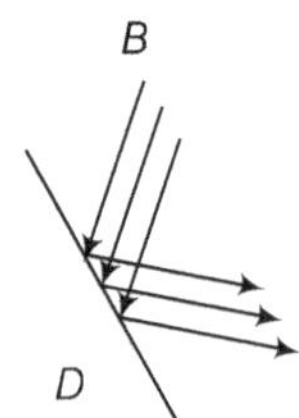

D

(a) Both *A* and *B* (b) *A, B* and *C*
(c) Only *D* (d) Only *B*

2. Which statement is not true in context with the figure given below?

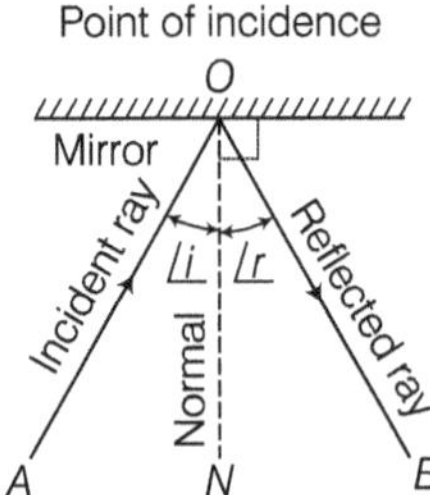

(a) $\angle AON = \angle BON$
(d) *AO* is the incident ray
(c) *O* is the only point from where the light ray can be reflected
(d) If *BO* is the incident ray, then *OA* will be the reflected ray

3. Which of these are characteristics of diffused reflection?

   I. Reflected rays go in one direction.
   II. Reflected rays are not parallel to each other.
   III. It is caused by irregularities of the reflecting surface.

   Codes
   (a) I and II
   (b) II and III
   (c) Only I
   (d) Only II

4. The figure shows a ray of light reflected at a plane mirror. Which pair of the angles of incidence and angles of reflection is correct?

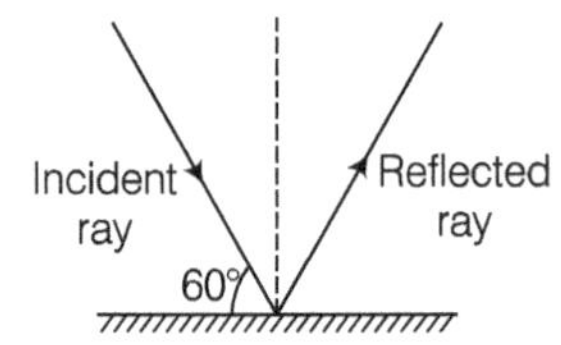

	Angle of incidence	Angle of reflection
(a)	30°	30°
(b)	30°	60°
(c)	60°	30°
(d)	60°	45°

5. A doll is placed between two parallel plane mirrors separated by 60 cm. How many images of the doll will be formed?

(a) 60   (b) 90   (c) 120   (d) Infinite

6. If the angle between incident ray and surface is 40° as shown in figure. What will be the angle of reflection?

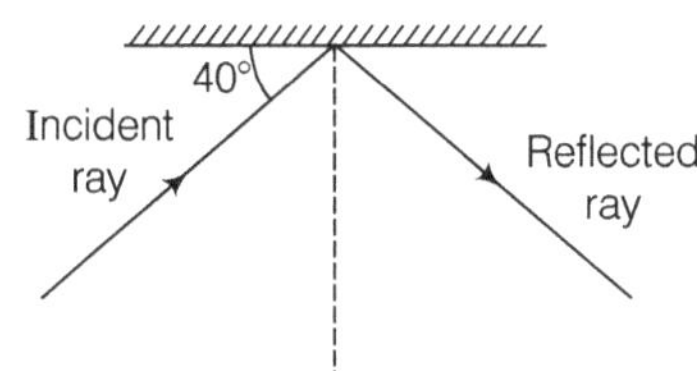

(a) 30°   (b) 40°
(c) 50°   (d) 60°

7. Light is falling on surfaces S_1, S_2, S_3 as shown in figures

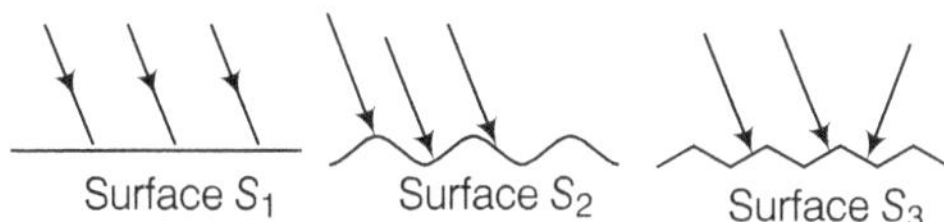

Surfaces on which the angle of incidence is equal to the angle of reflection is/are?

(a) Only S_1
(b) Both S_1 and S_2
(c) Both S_2 and S_3
(d) All the three surfaces

8. The image in a plane mirror is

I. upright

II. real

III. the same sized as the object

IV. as far behind the mirror as the object is in front of it.

Codes

(a) Only I   (b) I, II and III
(c) I, III and IV   (d) All of these

9. An optician holds a test card 50 cm behind a patient. The patient, then looks in the plane mirror which is 100 cm away. How far away from the patients eye is the image of test card?

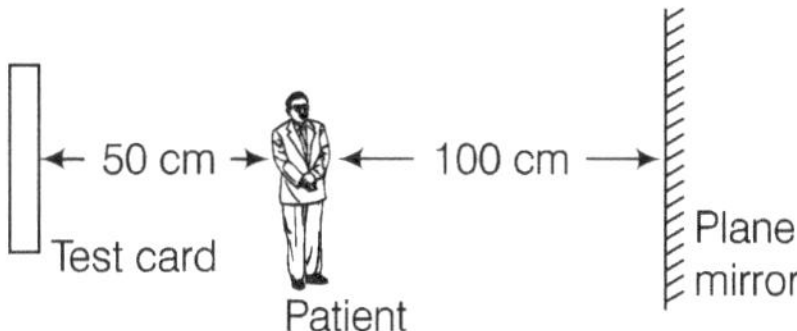

(a) 100 cm   (b) 150 cm
(c) 200 cm   (d) 250 cm

10. A man looked into a plane mirror and saw the clock as shown. The time on the clock was

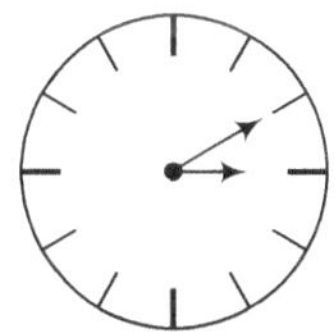

(a) 8 : 50   (b) 9 : 10
(c) 3 : 10   (d) 3 : 50

11. Which optical phenomenon is depicted in the figure below?

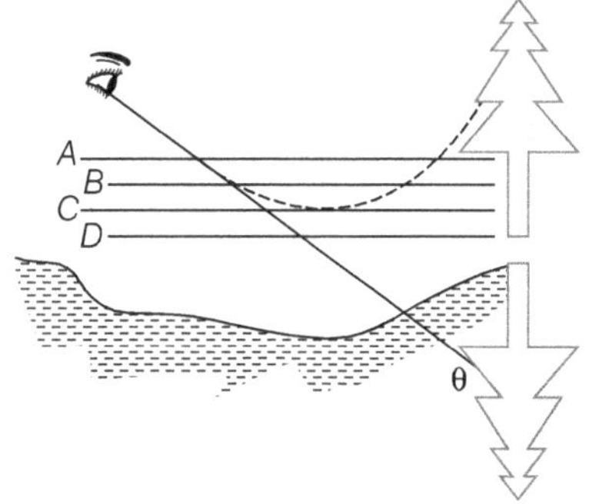

(a) Reflection of light
(b) Dispersion of light
(c) Scattering of light
(d) Refraction of light

12. With reference to the figure shown in above question, what is the cause of this optical illusion?
(a) Density of air decreases with increase of height.
(b) Density of air increases with height.
(c) Refractive index of air decreases with increase of height.
(d) Earth acts like a mirror.

13. The change in focal length of an eye lens to focus the image of objects at varying distances is done by the action of
(a) pupil (b) iris
(c) retina (d) ciliary muscles

14. When we enter into a dark room, we cannot see properly for some time. This is because
(a) pupil does not close
(b) pupil does not open
(c) adjustment of size of pupil takes some time
(d) None of the above

15. Which of the following statements is correct regarding rods and cones in human eye?
(a) Cones are sensitive to dim light.
(b) Cones are sensitive to coloured light.
(c) Rods are sensitive to bright light.
(d) Rods can sense colour.

16. A list of lenses is given below:
I. Concave lens

II. Convex lens

III. Plano–concave lens

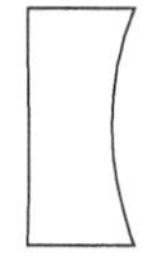

IV. Plano–convex lens

What kind of lens is there in our eyes?
(a) I (b) II (c) III (d) IV

17. The human eye can focus objects at different distances by adjusting the focal length of the eye lens.
This is due to
(a) presbyopia
(b) near-sightedness
(c) accommodation
(d) far-sightedness

18. The eye lens is a flexible lens whose thickness and focal length can be changed by the action of ciliary muscles. The focal length of the eye lens increases when eye muscles
(a) are relaxed and lens becomes thicker
(b) contract and lens becomes thicker
(c) are relaxed and lens becomes thinner
(d) contract and lens becomes thinner

19. Which of the following statement(s) about human eye is/are correct?
I. The iris is the outer coat of the eye.
II. It is behind the pupil.
III. Iris controls the adjustment of size of pupil.
IV. Iris is the coloured part of the eye.
Codes
(a) I and II (b) Only II
(c) II and III (d) III and IV

20. State [T] for true and [F] for false.

   I. Rods sense colour.

   II. Cones are sensitive to bright light.

   III. Rods are sensitive to dim light.

   IV. Cones function in dim light.

   Codes

	I	II	III	IV			I	II	III	IV
(a)	T	T	T	F	(b)		F	F	T	T
(c)	T	F	F	T	(d)		F	T	T	F

21. Which of the following statements is/are correct?

   Statement I It is difficult to thread a needle with one eye closed in comparison with keeping both eyes open.

   Statement II A human eye cannot see an object clearly for an object placed at a distance smaller than a certain minimum distance.

   (a) Only I   (b) Only II
   (c) Both I and II   (d) None of these

22. Which of the following statements is/are correct?

   Statement I Cinematography is an application of persistence of vision.

   Statement II (R) The retina of human eye has an ability to retain the image of an object for one-sixteenth of a second even after the removal of the object.

   (a) Only statement I is correct.
   (b) Only statement II is correct.
   (c) Both statements are correct.
   (d) Both statements are incorrect.

2 Marks Questions

23. A list of objects is given below:

   (i) Sun (ii) Moon (iii) Earth (iv) Stars

   (v) Glowing tubelight (vi) Table (vii) Fire

   Category I Luminous objects

   Category II Non-luminous objects

   What is the correct division of the given list of objects according to the two categories given?

   (a) I : (i), (ii), (iii), (iv)
        II : (v), (vi), (vii)
   (b) I : (i), (iv), (v), (vii)
        II : (ii), (iii), (vi)
   (c) I : (i), (ii), (iv)
        II : (iii), (v), (vi), (vii)
   (d) I : (i), (iv), (vii)
        II : (ii), (iii), (v), (vi)

24. Match the following columns.

	Column I		Column II
A.	Point of incidence	1.	Ray of light which is incident on the surface of mirror
B.	Reflected ray	2.	Perpendicular drawn at the point of incidence
C.	Incident ray	3.	Ray of light which bounces off the mirror
D.	Normal at the point of incidence	4.	Point where the incident ray strikes the surface of the mirror

   Codes

	A	B	C	D			A	B	C	D
(a)	4	3	1	2	(b)		1	3	2	4
(c)	3	4	1	2	(d)		4	1	2	3

I. Dispersion of light causes rainbow.

II. Diffused reflection of light occurs due to failure of the laws of reflection.

III. Image formed by a plane mirror is always laterally inverted.

Codes

	I	II	III			I	II	III
(a)	T	T	T		(b)	T	F	T
(c)	F	T	T		(d)	T	F	F

26. Match the following columns.

Column I	Column II
A. Diffused Reflection	1. Smooth surface
B. Regular reflection	2. Three plane mirror strips inclined at 60° to one another
C. Periscope	3. Irregular surface.
D. Kaleidoscope	4. Two plane mirrors arranged parallel to one another.

Codes

	A	B	C	D			A	B	C	D
(a)	1	3	2	4		(b)	1	3	4	2
(c)	3	1	2	4		(d)	3	1	4	2

27. State [T] for True and [F] for False.

I. A person of 1m long in front of a plane mirror seems to be 1 m from the image.

II. If you touch your left ear with right hand in front of a plane mirror, it will be seen in the mirror that your right ear is touched with left hand.

III. Splitting of white light into its constituent colours is known as diffraction.

IV. According to the laws of reflection, $\angle i$ less than $\angle r$.

Codes

	I	II	III	IV			I	II	III	IV
(a)	T	F	T	F		(b)	T	T	F	F
(c)	T	F	T	T		(d)	T	T	T	F

28. Match the following columns.

Column I	Column II
A. Cataract	1. Junction of optic nerve and retina
B. Cornea	2. Cloudy eye lens
C. Blind spot	3. 1/16th of a second
D. Persistence of vision	4. Front part of eye

Codes

	A	B	C	D			A	B	C	D
(a)	4	1	3	2		(b)	4	2	1	3
(c)	2	4	1	3		(d)	2	4	3	1

29. State (T) for true and (F) for False.

I. The most comfortable distance of clear reading with normal vision is approximately 25 cm.

II. The size of the pupil becomes small when you see in dim light.

III. Night birds have more cones than rods in their eyes.

IV. The image is formed at retina of an eye.

V. Cinematography works on the principle of reflection of light.

Codes

	I	II	III	IV	V
(a)	T	F	F	T	F
(b)	T	F	T	F	T
(c)	F	F	T	T	F
(d)	F	T	F	F	F

Stars and Solar System

1 Mark Questions

1. Stars are the celestial objects that are extremely hot and have light of their own. Stars emit heat and light continuously. What is the cause of production of heat and light by stars?
   (a) Nuclear fission
   (b) Nuclear fusion
   (c) Both (a) and (b)
   (d) Neither (a) nor (b)

2. The colour of a star comes from its temperatures. A star which appears blue will be
   (a) as hot as sun
   (b) cooler than sun
   (c) very cold indeed
   (d) much hotter than sun

3. Which of the following constellations can be seen in the night sky during the winter season?
   I. Orion   II. Ursa major
   III. Leo major   IV. Cassiopeia
   Codes
   (a) I and II
   (b) I and IV
   (c) II and III
   (d) II and IV

4. Which of the following figures depicts the position of pole star correctly?

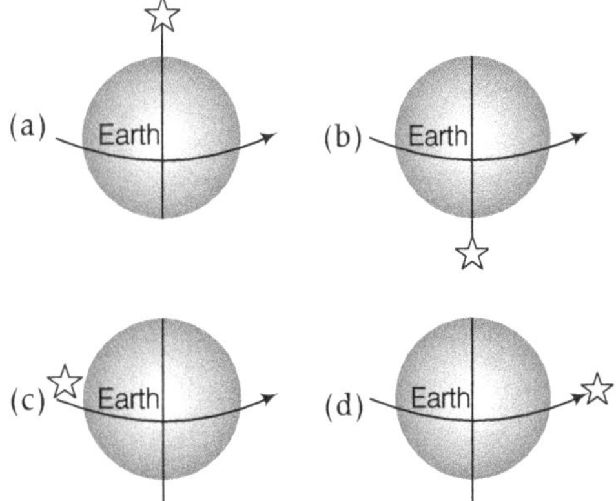

5. A list of names of constellations is given below:
   I. Big Dipper
   II. Saptarishi
   III. Great Bear
   IV. Plough
   V. Big Bear
   VI. Ursa Minor

   Choose the odd one out.
   (a) I   (b) III
   (c) IV   (d) VI

6. If we say a star is 10 light years away from earth, it means that
   (a) the light from that star takes 10 years to reach earth surface
   (b) the star which appears to us now is in fact the way it looked 10 years ago
   (c) Both (a) and (b)
   (d) Neither (a) nor (b)

7. Which of these differences are correct?

	A	B
P.	Planets have their own light	Stars reflect the light of the sun
Q.	Planets keep changing their position	Stars have a fixed position
R.	Planets orbit around the sun	Stars orbit around the planets

Codes
(a) *P* and *Q*
(b) *P* and *R*
(c) *Q* and *R*
(d) Only *Q*

8. Sun appears to move in the sky from East to west direction. Stars also appear to change their positions during the night because
   (a) of the rotation of earth on its axis
   (b) of the revolution of earth around the sun
   (c) stars are moving away from each other continuously
   (d) stars are moving towards each other continuously

9. Asteroids are small celestial objects which revolve around the sun. Where would you find asteroids if you were orbiting the solar system?
   (a) Between Mars and Jupiter
   (b) Between Earth and Venus
   (c) Between Mars and Mercury
   (d) Between Venus and Jupiter

10. Which of the following planets have no moon?
    I. Venus   II. Mars
    III. Mercury   IV. Jupiter
    V. Neptune
    Codes
    (a) I and II
    (b) I and III
    (c) II and IV
    (d) III and V

11. Which of the following figure shown as *A*, *B*, *C* and *D* below is not a member of the solar system?

A. Saturn

B. Comet

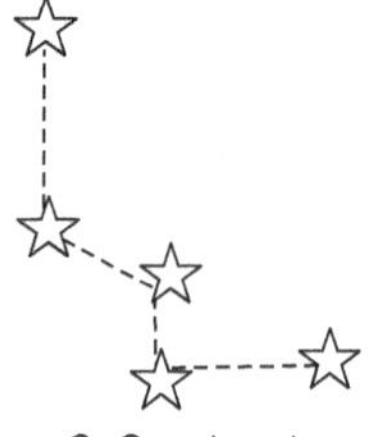

C. Cassiopeia

D. Asteroids

(a) *A*   (b) *B*   (c) *C*   (d) *D*

12. According to the chart, on which planet would a ball fall the fastest?

Planet	Earth	Jupiter	Neptune	Saturn
Acceleration due to gravity	10	26	14	12

(a) Jupiter
(b) Saturn
(c) Neptune
(d) Earth

13. Seasons on Earth keep on changing. The change in seasons on the Earth occurs because
    (a) the distance between the Earth and the sun is not constant
    (b) the axis of rotation of the Earth is parallel to the plane of its orbit

(c) the axis of rotation of the Earth is perpendicular to the plane of its orbit

(d) the axis of rotation of the Earth is tilted with respect of the plane of its orbit

14. The different appearances of the bright, visible part of the Moon as seen from the Earth over the whole month are called phases of the Moon. Phases of the moon occur because

(a) we can see only that part of the moon which reflects light towards us

(b) our distance from the moon keeps changing

(c) the shadow of the earth covers only a part of a moon's surface

(d) the thickness of the moon's atmosphere is not constant

15. In the given figure, out of the positions *A*, *B*, *C* and *D* which will indicate the position of the sun?

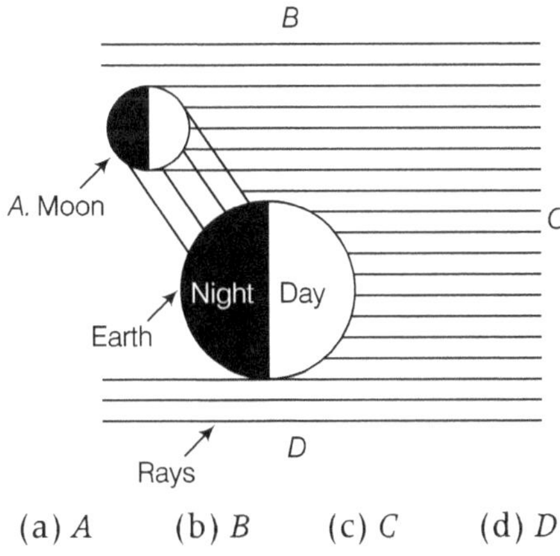

(a) *A*   (b) *B*   (c) *C*   (d) *D*

16. The first of a month is the new Moon day. On fifteenth of the same month, which of the following figures would represent the phase of the Moon?

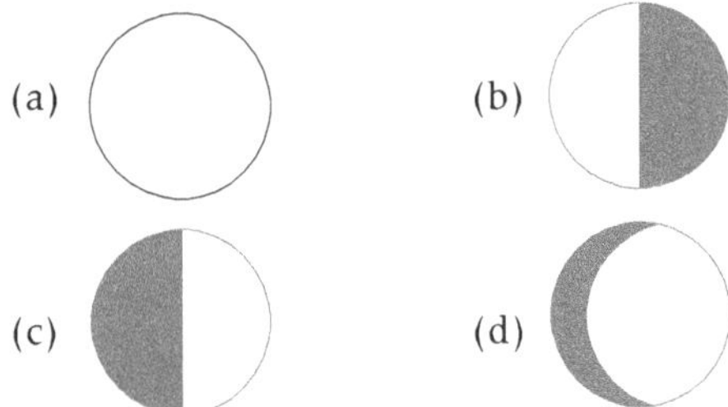

17. The Earth rotates around its axis. The Sun appears to rise in the east and set in the west. Venus rotates in the opposite direction of Earth. We can therefore assume that on Venus, the Sun sets in the

(a) East

(b) West

(c) North

(d) South

18. No matter how hard you look, you'll never find me, unless you have a telescope. I was once called a planet but not anymore. Now, I am just a dwarf planet but too important to ignore. Who am I?

(a) Mars

(b) Mercury

(c) Neptune

(d) Pluto

2 Marks Questions

19. X is a group of stars which is visible during the summer season in the early part of the night. It is clearly visible in the month of April in the Northern part of the sky. It resembles a big kite with a tail.

    What are two names of X. How many bright stars are usually observed in X?
    (a) Orion, Hunter, Eight
    (b) Orion, Big Dipper, Eight
    (c) Ursa Major, Hunter, Seven
    (d) Ursa Major, Great Bear, Seven

20. State [T] for true and [F] for false.
    I. Orion is called the little bear.
    II. The saptarishi appears like a hunter.
    III. The pole star can be located with the Ursa Major.
    IV. The pole star lies on the axis of rotation of the Earth.

    Codes

	I	II	III	IV
(a)	T	T	F	F
(b)	T	F	T	F
(c)	F	F	T	T
(d)	F	T	F	T

21. Which of the following statement(s) given below is/are incorrect?
    I. Meteors are not stars.
    II. Due to friction, meteors burn up in the sky.
    III. A meteor which reaches the earth's atmosphere is called an asteroid.
    IV. A planet is called shooting star.

    Codes
    (a) I and II   (b) Only II
    (c) Only III   (d) III and IV

22. Which of the following statements about a comet are incorrect?
    I. Comets revolve around the sun in highly elliptical orbits.
    II. A comet has a bright head and a long tail.
    III. The tail is always directed towards the sun.
    IV. The size of the head lengthens as it approaches the sun.

    Codes
    (a) I and II
    (b) II and III
    (c) I and III
    (d) III and IV

23. Taking one light year equal to 9.4×10^{15} m and one day equal to 86400 s, what will be the speed of light in light year per day if the speed of light in ms^{-1} is 3×10^{8}?
    (a) 2.75×10^{-3} ly day^{-1}
    (b) 3.75×10^{-3} ly day^{-1}
    (c) 2.75×10^{3} ly day^{-1}
    (d) 3.75×10^{3} ly day^{-1}

Pollution of Air and Water

1 Mark Questions

1. Given below is a food chain that exist in nature.

   Phytoplankton → *Moina* (water fleas) → Herring → Salmon → Eagle

   If a non-biodegradable insecticide like DDT gets added to water and enter this food chain, the highest concentration will be accumulated in
   (a) Phytoplankton   (b) Salmon
   (c) *Moina*   (d) Eagle

2. In a water sample taken from Yamuna river, the presence of *E. coli* in very level indicates the
   (a) hardness of water
   (b) pollution of water by sewage
   (c) softness of water
   (d) pollution of water by industrial effluents

3. If no carbon dioxide was present on the Earth's surface, the temperature of the Earth's surface would be
   (a) same as present
   (b) higher than present
   (c) lesser than present
   (d) depends on the oxygen level in atmosphere

4. A rise in the temperature of the Earth is directly associated with rise in sea level because
   I. More water in the atmosphere would condense, so more rainfall will occur.
   II. Sea water would expand because of increased heating.
   III. Ice caps and glaciers would melt.
   (a) I and II
   (b) Only II
   (c) Only I
   (d) Only III

5. Frogs and toads seem to be more affected by pollution in comparison to many other animals, including other amphibians. What might explain this?
   (a) They have to live in two environments, water and land, so they face two kinds of pollution
   (b) They tend to live in places throughout the world that are crowded with people
   (c) They have thin porous skin
   (d) They eat insects that are very dirty

6. Match the Column I with Column II.

	Column I		Column II
A.	Minamata disease	1.	Arsenic
B.	Blackfoot disease	2.	Mercury
C.	Cancer of liver and lungs	3.	Bacteria
D.	Cholera	4.	Cadmium

Codes

	A	B	C	D		A	B	C	D
(a)	2	1	3	4	(b)	2	1	4	3
(c)	1	2	3	4	(d)	3	1	2	4

7. Read the statements w.r.t a gaseous pollutant X given below.

I. It has no colour.

II. It has no taste or odour.

III. It is a radioactive noble gas.

IV. It contributes to air pollution.

Mark the option that corresponds to the above statements.

(a) Carbon   (b) Sulphur

(c) Radon   (d) Xenon

8. The marine life in the ocean was badly affected by an oil spill. A lot of fish and other marine animals were found dead and floating on the surface of water. This is because ....

I. They drank the water which was contaminated by oil.

II. The fish swallowed the oil droplets and were contaminated.

III. They breathed in the oil fumes and were suffocated.

Codes

(a) Only I   (b) I and II

(c) II and III   (d) I, II and III

9. Study the given Venn diagram. X is likely to be......... .

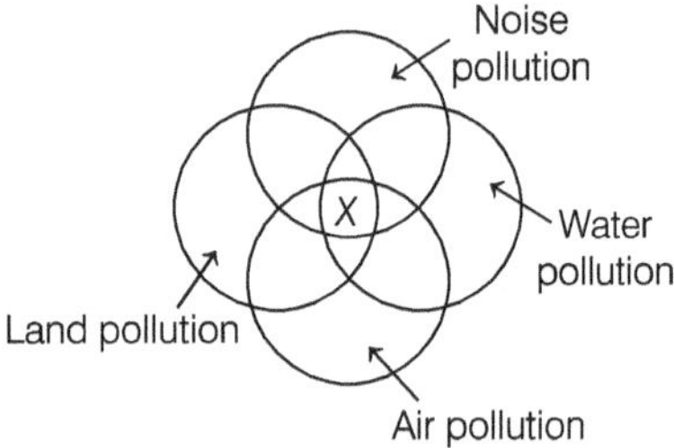

(a) a group of people smoking cigarettes

(b) youngsters dancing in a disco

(c) a farmer spraying pesticides near a river

(d) construction work going on at a building site

10. Which of the following procedure will give you water free from all impurities?

(a) Adding chlorine tablets

(b) Distillation

(c) Boiling

(d) Filtration

11. Madhav collects the fallen dry leaves from his lawn and he disposes them into a compost pit instead of burning. This will help in

(a) reducing water pollution

(b) reducing air pollution

(c) reducing the soil fertility

(d) None of the above

12. Vedika's father has an old car which causes more air pollution due to burning of petrol. What should he use to prevent air pollution?

(a) Diesel

(b) CNG

(c) LPG

(d) All of the above

13. Global warming can be controlled by
(a) reducing reforestation and increasing the consumption of fossil fuels
(b) increasing deforestation and reducing efficiency of energy usage
(c) reducing deforestation and cutting down use fossil fuels
(d) stop using fossil fuels completely

14. Taj Mahal, one of the seven wonders of the world is known for the beauty of its snow white marble but due to the effect of acid rain its brightness is fading and its marble is corroded.

What this phenomenon is called and which court has taken some beneficial steps to protect the beauty of Taj Mahal?

	Phenomenon	**Court**
(a)	Acid cancer	High court
(b)	Marble cancer	Supreme court
(c)	Sangamarmar cancer	High court
(d)	Acid marble cancer	Supreme court

15. In the given flow chart wastewater treatment is described. But some of the steps in the flow chart are incorrectly arranged. Consider the chart carefully and select the correct sequence

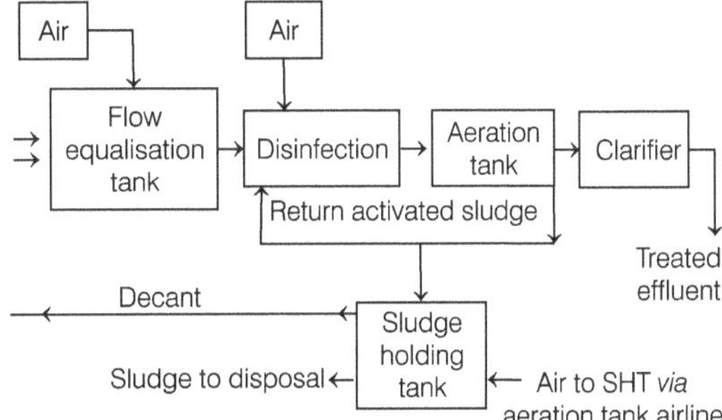

(a) Flow equalisation tank – aeration tank – clarifier – disinfection
(b) Aeration tank – flow equalisation tank – disinfection – clarifier
(c) Clarifier – disinfection – flow equalisation tank – aeration tank
(d) Disinfection – flow equalisation tank – clarifier – aeration tank

2 Marks Questions

16. Trees are planted along the roadside to reduce pollution from motor vehicles. They reduce pollution by
 I. Absorbing traffic noise.
 II. Taking in carbon dioxide.
 III. Trapping dust and root from the exhaust pipes of vehicle.
 IV. Enhancing the level of noise generated.

Codes
(a) I, II and III
(b) II and IV
(c) III and IV
(d) All of these

17. Select the pair which is incorrectly matched.
(a) Potable water–Water free from impurities and microorganisms.
(b) BOD–The amount of oxygen required to oxidise all the reducing substances present in water.
(c) Oil spills–Accidental discharges of petroleum from oil tankers and oil refineries in water bodies.
(d) Eutrophication–Enrichment of water by nutrients which leads to excessive plant growth and depletion of dissolved oxygen.

18. Consider the following statements and select the option which correctly identifies true (T) and false (F).

    I. Instead of coal and petroleum, solar energy, hydro power and wind energy and can be used as alternatives fuels.

    II. Excess greenhouse gases present in the atmosphere releases a lot of heat and leads to cooling of Earth's surface.

    III. Smog is formed by condensation of water vapour with H_2S and SO_2 over dust or smoke particles.

    IV. Kyoto protocol was signed to reduce the emission of greenhouse gases.

    Codes

	I	II	III	IV			I	II	III	IV
(a)	T	F	T	F		(b)	T	F	F	T
(c)	F	F	T	T		(d)	T	F	T	T

19. Mary uses the water that was used to do the laundry to wash the floor. Which of the following statements are correct about her action?

    I. She saves water by reusing the water.

    II. She is increasing the wastage of clean water.

    III. She saves water by reducing the use of clean water.

    IV. She saves water by recycling the water that was used to do laundry.

    Codes
    (a) I and III
    (b) II and IV
    (c) I, III and IV
    (d) II, III and IV

PRACTICE SET 01

1 Mark Questions

1. Which of the following factors affect the natural habitat of endemic species?
   - I. Destruction of their habitat.
   - II. Increasing human population.
   - III. Introduction of new species.
   - IV. Introduction of same species.
   - (a) I and II
   - (b) II and III
   - (c) I, II and III
   - (d) I, .II, III and IV

2. Match the items given in Column I with their suitable match given in Column II and choose the correct answer using the codes given below.

	Column I		Column II
A.	Mercury	1.	Turns red litmus blue
B.	Carbon dioxide	2.	Exist in liquid state
C.	Gold	3.	Can be beaten into sheets
D.	Magnesium oxide	4.	Can be cut with a sharp knife
		5.	Turns blue litmus red

   Codes

	A	B	C	D			A	B	C	D
(a)	2	1	3	5		(b)	2	1	4	5
(c)	2	5	4	1		(d)	2	5	3	1

3. The given below diagram shows a rubber tyre.

   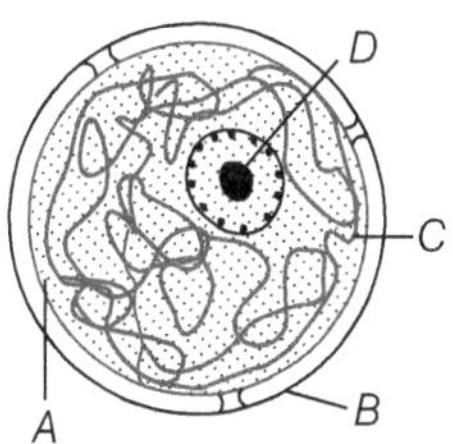

   There are deep treads on the tyre because they
   - (a) increase the slipping distance of the car
   - (b) reduce the amount of material used
   - (c) enable the tyre to move smoothly
   - (d) increase friction

4. The following diagram shows an oil well with natural gas, oil and water.

   Oil and gas form the upper layer. This is because

   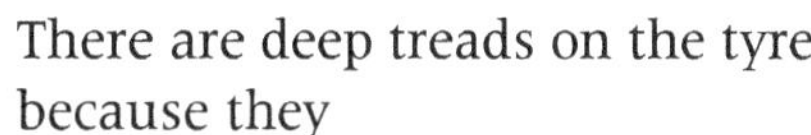

   - (a) these are heavier than water
   - (b) these are lighter than water
   - (c) these get stick to each other
   - (d) these mix with water

5. The force of friction between two bodies is
   - (a) parallel to the contact surfaces
   - (b) perpendicular to the contact surfaces
   - (c) inclined at $30°$ to the contact surfaces
   - (d) inclined at $60°$ to the contact surfaces

6. Observe the given structure of nucleus and opt the part that will lead to formation of chromosomes.

   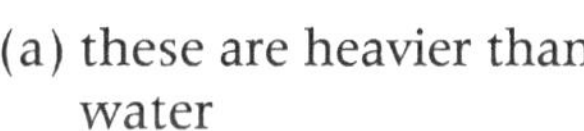

   Codes
   - (a) B
   - (b) C
   - (c) A
   - (d) D

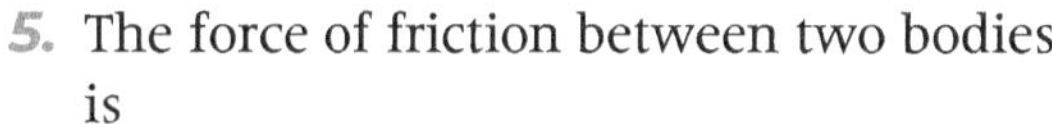

7. Which of the following is the best thing to do during heavy lightning?
(a) Lying on the ground in an open place
(b) Going into the nearest water body
(c) Staying indoors away from metallic doors or windows
(d) Standing under a tall tree

8. Rohan took a magnesium ribbon and burnt it in air.

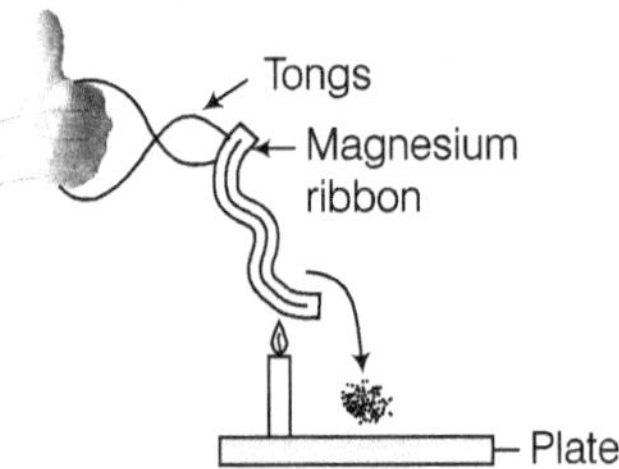

The product(s) obtained during this experiment is/are

I. Magnesium oxide

II. Magnesium nitride

III. Magnesium carbonate

(a) Only I　　　　(b) Only II
(c) I and II　　　(d) I, II and III

9. Match the following columns.

	Column I		Column II
A.	Point of incidence	1.	Ray of light which is incident on the surface of mirror
B.	Reflected ray	2.	Perpendicular drawn at the point of incidence
C.	Incident ray	3.	Ray of light which bounces off the mirror
D.	Normal at the point of incidence	4.	Point where the incident ray strikes the surface of the mirror

Codes

	A	B	C	D
(a)	4	3	1	2
(b)	1	3	2	4
(c)	3	4	1	2
(d)	4	1	2	3

10. Two different cells are given as cell I and II. The observations are as follow.

Trait	Cell I	Cell II
Cell wall	Present	Present
Ribosome	Present	Present
Nucleus	Absent	Present
Ability to photosynthesis	Present	Absent
Cell respiration	Present	Present

These observations support which of the following conclusions?
(a) Cell I is more complex in its organisation than cell II.
(b) Cell I is a prokaryote.
(c) The ancestors of cell II appeared earlier in the fossil records than the ancestors of cell I.
(d) Both the cells are plant cells.

11. A man sharpens his knife as shown in the figure. Which of these properties of friction are in use?

I. Friction helps us to hold objects.

II. Friction acts in the opposite direction of motion.

III. Friction causes the surfaces in contact to wear away.

IV. Friction produces heat energy.

Codes
(a) I and II
(b) I, III and IV
(c) III and IV
(d) I, II and III

12. Which of the following are negative effects of deforestation on the environment?

   I. Destruction of the ozone layer.

  II. Erosion of the topsoil.

 III. Increase in carbon dioxide level.

Codes

(a) Only I   (b) Only II
(c) II and III   (d) I, II and III

13. Some students were performing experiment in the laboratory. One step of their experiment involve heating of alcohol. However, their science teacher strictly instructed them not to heat the alcohol directly on the flame.

Why do you think, the teacher gave such an instruction?

   I. The temperature of the flame is not high enough to heat the alcohol.

  II. Alcohol is highly inflammable substance.

 III. The heat of the flame is sufficient to overcome the ignition temperature of alcohol, so it can easily catch fire.

The correct reason(s) is/are

(a) I and II   (b) II and III
(c) I and III   (d) Only III

14. Opt the correct level of organisation.

(a) Cell → Tissue → Organ → Organ system → Organism
(b) Tissue → Cell → Organ → Organ system → Organism
(c) Cell → Tissue → Organ system → Organ → Organism
(d) Cell → Organ → Tissue → Organ system → Organism

15. To avoid slipping while walking on ice, we should take smaller steps because

(a) frictional force of ice is large
(b) of larger normal reaction
(c) frictional force of ice is small
(d) of smaller normal reaction

16. Mr. Verma wrote the following statements about elements X, Y and Z.

   I. X is stored under kerosene oil.

  II. Y catches fire when exposed to air, so stored under water.

 III. Z reacts with water slowly.

Then he told the students to identify X, Y and Z. Can you guess what are X, Y and Z?

(a) Sodium, magnesium, copper
(b) Sodium, phosphorus, iron
(c) Copper, zinc, potassium
(d) Zinc, copper, sodium

17. Opt the option involved in the detoxification or removal of toxic substances from the cell.

(a) Golgi bodies
(b) Smooth endoplasmic reticulum
(c) Lysosomes
(d) Centrosomes

18. Radhika is observing a satellite with the help of a telescope that does not appear to move in the sky. In which orbit is this satellite placed?

(a) Polar   (b) Eccentric
(c) Low Earth   (d) Geo-stationary

19. What benefit does yeast gains from carrying out fermentation?

(a) Carbon dioxide is available for photosynthesis.
(b) Energy is available for growth.
(c) Ethanol is available for growth.
(d) Glucose is available for respiration.

20. The diagrams represent samples of bacteria growing in a dish of a nutrient. Diagram 2 shows the sample after three hours.

Bacteria t = 0 h   Bacteria t = 3 h

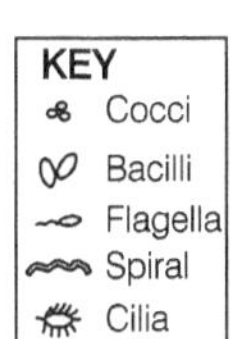

Diagram 1   Diagram 2

Which type of bacterium is multiplying the fastest?
(a) Cocci
(b) Bacilli
(c) Spiral
(d) Cilia

21. Select the correct statement.
    (a) The force of friction depends on the area of the surfaces in contact.
    (b) Rolling friction is less than sliding friction.
    (c) More the weight, less the frictional force.
    (d) Friction produces energy.

22. The correct sequence and components of crude oil after fractional distillation of petroleum is

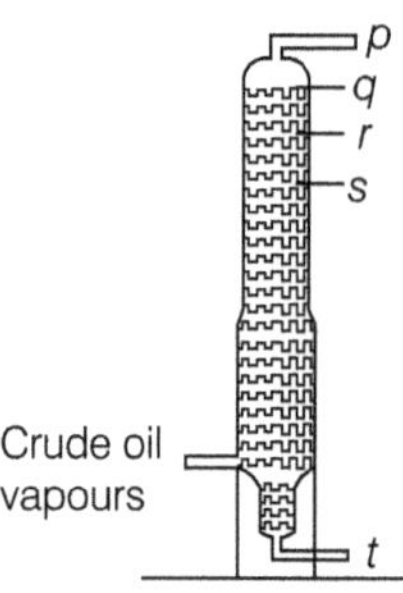

    (a) p–Residue, q–Gasoline, r–Petroleum gases, s–Kerosene, t–Diesel oil
    (b) p–Petroleum gases, q–Gasoline, r–Diesel oil, s–Kerosene, t–Residue
    (c) p–Petroleum gases, q–Gasoline, r–Kerosene, s–Diesel oil, t–Residue
    (d) p–Petroleum gases, q–Kerosene, r–Gasoline, s–Diesel oil, t–Residue

23. Consider the given statements and opt the option that correctly declares them true (T) or false (F).
    I. Sodium bicarbonate is an antibiotic.
    II. The first antibiotic called penicillin was extracted from fungus.
    III. Sodium hydroxide can be used as a food preservative.
    IV. Fungus are normally considered as saprophytes.

Codes

	I	II	III	IV
(a)	F	T	F	T
(b)	T	T	F	T
(c)	F	T	T	F
(d)	T	T	T	T

24. The four activities (A, B, C and D) below show forces at work.

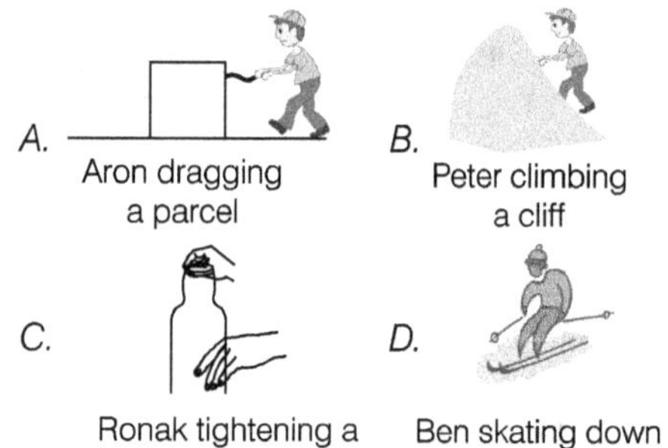

    Which of the following activities require the presence of frictional force?
    (a) Activities A and B
    (b) Activities B and C
    (c) Activities A and C
    (d) All the activities

25. Read the following statements about cotton.
    I. Cotton is very strong.
    II. Cotton is waterproof.
    III. Cotton creases easily.
    IV. Cotton is warm to wear.
    The correct statements are
    (a) I and II
    (b) III and IV
    (c) I and III
    (d) I and IV

26. DNA and RNA both found in which of the following parts?
    (a) Nucleus and cytoplasm, respectively
    (b) Cell wall
    (c) Cell sap
    (d) Vacuole

27. Refer to the given Venn diagram and choose the correct option for X and Y.

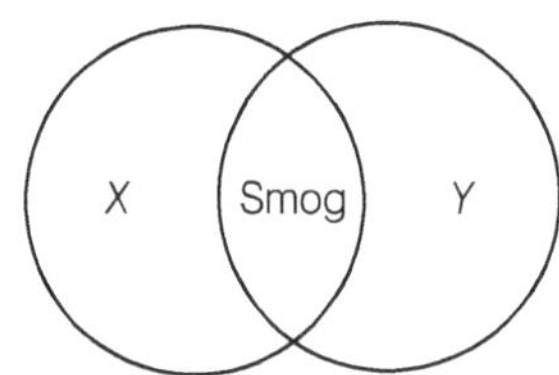

X	Y
(a) Fire	Water
(b) Smoke	Fog
(c) Water	Smoke
(d) Air	Water

28. Consider the following statements about an element X.

I. It is a very reactive element.

II. It releases hydrogen with dilute nitric acid.

III. It burns with white dazzling light.

Element X is

(a) sodium   (b) magnesium
(c) phosphorus   (d) calcium

29. Which of the following statements about friction is correct?
(a) Friction can be increased by moisture on the surface.
(b) Motion opposes friction.
(c) It is not possible to write without friction.
(d) Solids and liquids do not allow things to move in or over them.

30. Rahul took three samples of clothes and marked them A, B and C. He holded each sample by the tongs and burn into the flame.

The results observed by him are as follow:

I. A and B burn with smell of burning hair and A left residue.

II. C burns quickly with the smell of burning paper.

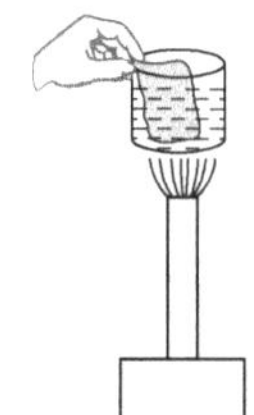
Burning of sample with the help of tongs

On the basis of his observation, he predicted that the fibres A, B and C respectively are
(a) wool, silk, cotton
(b) silk, nylon, rayon
(c) nylon, silk, cotton
(d) wool, nylon, acrylic

31. Which of the following is an example of a single cell that does not function as a full-fledged organism?
A. White Blood Cell (WBC)
B. *Amoeba*
C. WBC and *Amoeba*
D. *Paramecium*
(a) Only B   (b) B and D
(c) Only A   (d) C and D

32. Consider the following equations.
$$2A + 2B \longrightarrow 2AOH + H_2$$
$$S + O_2 \longrightarrow C$$
$$C + B \longrightarrow D$$

Here, A, B, C and D respectively are
(a) Na, H_2O, SO_2, H_2SO_3
(b) Na, H_2O, SO_2, H_2SO_4
(c) K, H_2O, SO_2, H_2SO_4
(d) K, H_2O, SO_3, H_2SO_3

33. Which of the following statement is incorrect?
(a) Alcohol is produced with the help of yeast.
(b) The food material which is preserved by pasteurisation is fruits and vegetables.
(c) The bread dough rises because of increased CO_2.
(d) The percentage of nitrogen gas in the atmosphere remains constant.

34. **Statement I** Stars appear to move from East to West direction.

Statement II Earth rotates from West to East causing Sun to rise from East and set in West.

Which of the following statement(s) is/are correct?
(a) Only I
(b) Only II
(c) Both I and II
(c) None of these

35. Match the following columns.

Column I		Column II
A. Coal	1.	Bus
B. Water in a dam	2.	Thermal power station
C. CNG	3.	Hydroelectric power station
D. Wind	4.	Cooking
E. LPG	5.	Wind mill

Codes

	A	B	C	D	E
(a)	1	2	3	4	5
(b)	2	3	5	4	1
(c)	2	3	1	5	4
(d)	3	1	2	5	4

36. Which of the following algae is used in making glasses and porcelain?
(a) *Chlorella*
(b) Diatoms
(c) Green algae
(d) *Volvox*

37. Select the incorrect statement.
(a) Angle of incidence is always equal to the angle of reflection.
(b) In an image formed by a mirror the left of the object appears on the right and *vice-versa*. This is known as lateral inversion.
(c) Reflection from a smooth surface is called diffused reflection.
(d) Cone cells sense colours.

38. Sources of energy are classified into two categories X and Y as shown below:

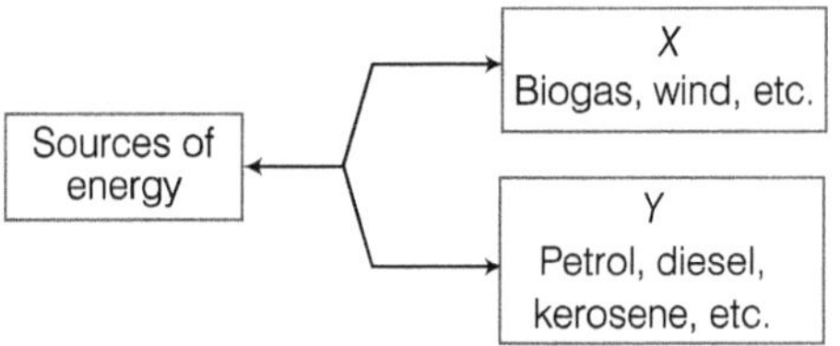

Which of these will go in Y?
(a) Liquefied Petroleum Gas
(b) Tides
(c) Coke
(d) All of the above

39. The microorganism in the given figure is

(a) Bread mould
(b) Penicillin
(c) Diatoms
(d) *Volvox*

40. X is an alloy and Y shows the elements from which it is made up of.

Rama has the following pairs for X and Y.

	X	Y
I.	Brass	Copper and zinc
II.	German silver	Silver and zinc
III.	Magnalium	Aluminium and tin
IV.	Bauxite	Copper and aluminium

The correct set(s) is/are
(a) I, II and III
(b) II and III
(c) Only I
(d) I and IV

2 Marks Questions

41. The given figure is a type of microscopic cell organelle which is found in all animal cells, but is most numerous in disease-fighting cells, such as white blood cells. This is because white blood cells must digest more material than other types of cells in their quest to battle bacteria, viruses and other foreign intruders. Identify this cell organelle.

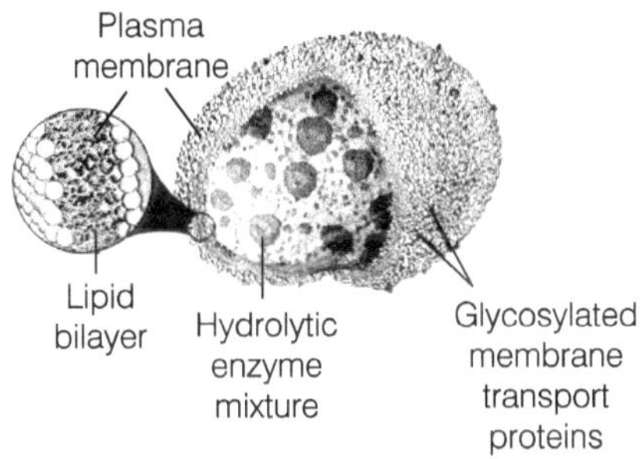

(a) Endoplasmic reticulum
(b) Mitochondria
(c) Lysosome
(d) Nucleus

42. Sonam performed the following experiment.

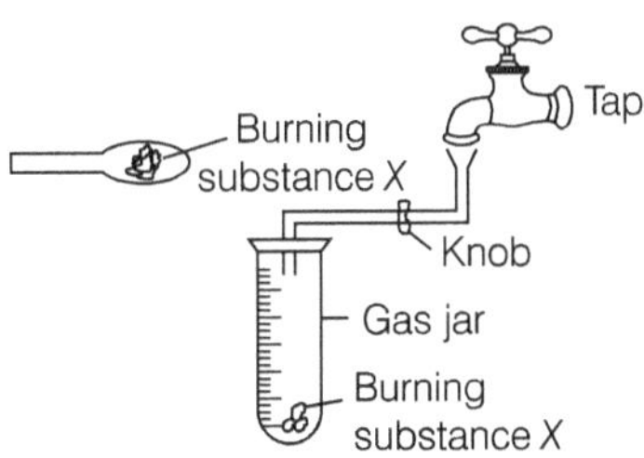

She added water to the jar by opening the knob, mixed the solution well and then remove the tube from the gas jar and put a few drops of the liquid over the red and blue litmus papers. The red litmus paper turns blue but blue litmus paper remains unaffected.

The burning substance X is
(a) magnesium   (b) sulphur
(c) phosphorus   (d) carbon

43. Parachute works because of air friction. If there was no air friction, then gravity would cause everything to fall at the same rate, so no matter what item you dropped like a feather or a rock it would hit the ground exactly at the same time (assuming you dropped it from the same height). But air friction complicates things. Air friction comes into action because as things fall, they have to push their way past the atoms and molecules that make up air in order to get their way to proceed.

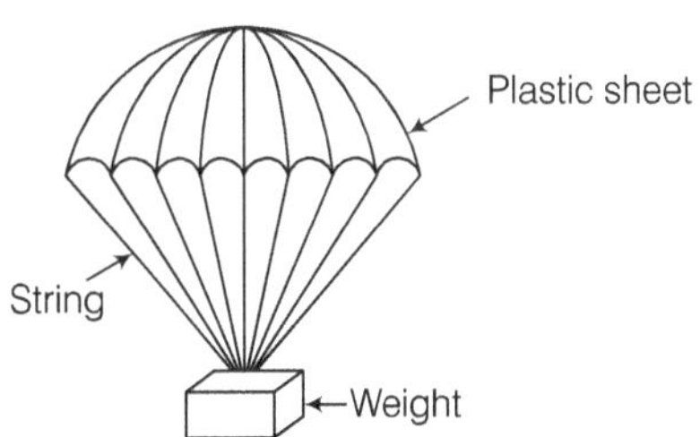

What force acting on parachute caused it to fall to the ground?
(a) Magnetic force
(b) Frictional force
(c) Gravitational force
(d) Both (b) and (c)

44. Ravi took two candles, one smaller and other slightly taller. He placed both the candles in a dish filled with baking soda and the dish is now placed in a large bowl as shown below.

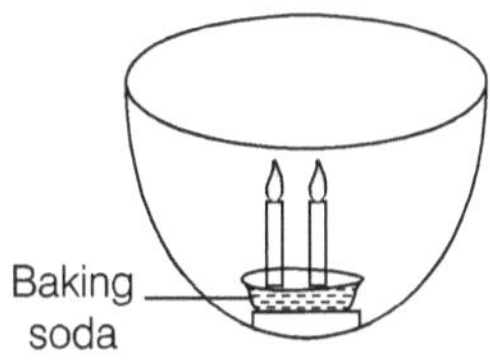

He now light up both the candles and pour vinegar into the dish of baking soda carefully so that it does not fall over the candles.

After some time, he observed that both the candles get extinguished. First smaller candle extinguish and later the larger one.

Why the candles get extinguished?
(a) Because of the production of water which cuts the supply of air by covering the fire.
(b) Because of carbon dioxide gas produced which cuts the supply of air (oxygen) by covering the fire.
(c) Because of nitrogen gas produced, which cuts the supply of air by covering the fire.
(d) Both (a) and (b)

45. A plant cell and an animal cell are shown below.

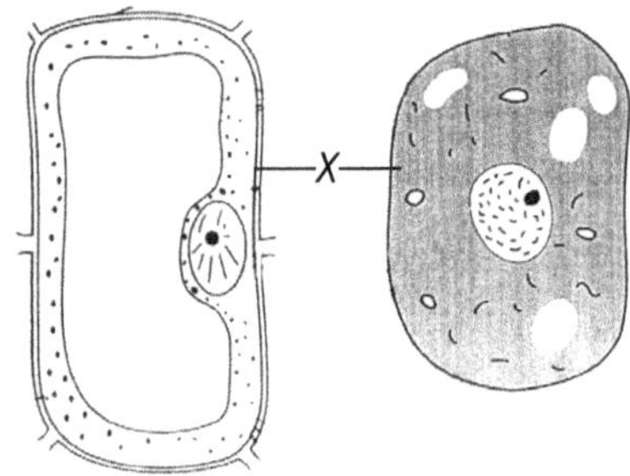

What does X represent?
(a) Nucleus
(b) Cytoplasm
(c) Cell membrane
(d) Cell wall

46. Under normal working conditions, radio loudspeakers, industrial machinery and children in a playground, all produce sound waves. Under the same air conditions, all these sound waves
(a) have the same amplitude
(b) have the same frequency
(c) have the same wavelength
(d) travel with same speed

47. In order to show the classification of fossil fuels, Mr. Verma, the science teacher draw the following flow chart.

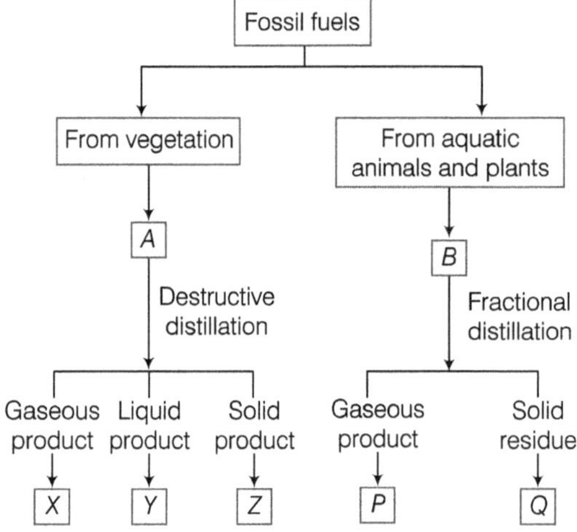

The set showing correct match for the vacant spaces $(A, B, X, Y, Z, P$ and $Q)$ is
(a) $A =$ Petroleum, $Y =$ Coal tar, $Q =$ Coke
(b) $X =$ Coal gas, $Z =$ Coke, $Q =$ Bitumen
(c) $B =$ Petroleum, $Z =$ Coke, $P =$ Gasoline
(d) $A =$ Coal, $X =$ Coal tar, $Q =$ Gasoline

48. Match the following columns.

	Column I		Column II
A.	AIDS	1.	Fungus
B.	Ringworm	2.	Protozoa
C.	Malaria	3.	Virus
D.	Whooping cough	4.	Bacteria

Codes

	A	B	C	D
(a)	1	3	4	2
(b)	2	4	3	1
(c)	3	1	2	4
(d)	3	2	4	1

49. The diagram below shows a planet at various positions as it orbits around the sun. The areas *W, X, Y* and *Z* are all equal to each other.

The planet takes the same amount of time to move from P1 to P2, from P3 to P4, from P5 to P6 and from P7 to P8.

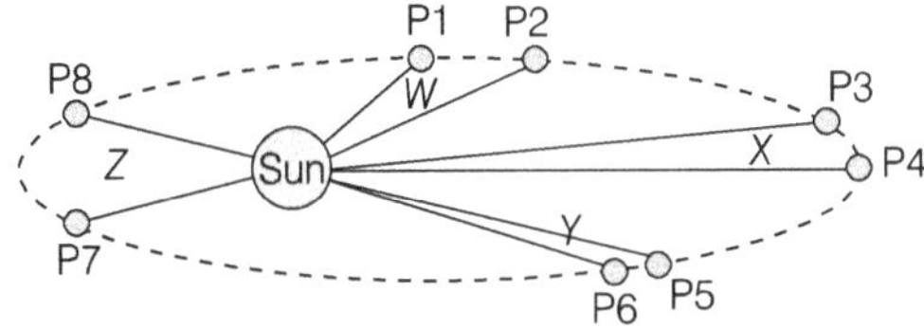

The speed of the planet is greatest as it travels from
(a) P1 to P2
(b) P3 to P4
(c) P5 to P6
(d) P7 to P8

50. Consider the statements given below and opt the option that declares them correctly either true (T) or false (F).

    I. Prokaryotic cells do not have cell nucleus.

   II. Genes are responsible for inheritance.

  III. An electron microscope magnifies objects over 500,000 times.

  IV. Cells arise from nutrients.

   V. Chromosomes are made up of DNA.

Codes

	I	II	III	IV	V
(a)	T	T	F	F	T
(b)	T	T	F	F	F
(c)	T	T	T	F	T
(d)	T	T	T	F	F

PRACTICE SET 

1 Mark Questions

1. Match the following columns.

	Column I		Column II
A.	Frictional force	1.	Comb with dry hair
B.	Electrostatic force	2.	Bullock pulling cart
C.	Muscular force	3.	Rolling ball
D.	Gravitational force	4.	Apple falling from tree

Codes

	A	B	C	D		A	B	C	D
(a)	1	4	3	2	(b)	2	3	1	4
(c)	3	1	2	4	(d)	3	2	1	4

2. Rahul pushes a wall for a very long time and gets tired. His muscles started aching but he still couldn't move the wall.

Which among the following statement is correct?

  I. No work is done by Rahul.

  II. Rahul spends a lot of his energy.

  III. Wall is stationary and cannot be moved.

  IV. Wall has a very ligh static friction.

Codes

(a) Only I   (b) Only II

(c) I, II and IV   (d) I, II, III and IV

3. Identify the incorrect statement from the following with reference to mitochondria.

(a) They are found both in plant and animal cells.

(b) Their inner membrane has projections called cristae.

(c) They contain different kinds of colouring pigments.

(d) They are involved in storage and release of energy.

4. Select the correct match.

(a) Lightning conductor → Electric current

(b) Seismic zones → Weak

(c) Moving charges → Earthquake

(d) Earth's plate → Protection

5. Match the items given in Column I with their most suitable match given in Column II and choose the correct answer using the codes given below.

	Column I		Column II
A.	LPG	1.	Plastic
B.	CNG	2.	Petroleum gas in liquid form
C.	Conversion of coal into coke	3.	Natural gas
D.	Petroleum	4.	Coal gas
		5.	Produces gas

Codes

	A	B	C	D		A	B	C	D
(a)	4	3	5	1	(b)	2	3	5	1
(c)	2	4	5	1	(d)	2	3	4	1

6. Statement I Prokaryotes have a cell wall, whereas in eukaryotes, it is absent.

Statement II Prokaryotes have a true nucleus while eukaryotes have a primitive nucleus.

Which of the following statement(s) is/are correct?
(a) Only I   (b) Only II
(c) Both I and II   (d) None of these

7. Which of the following cannot be charged easily by friction?
   (a) A plastic scale
   (b) A copper rod
   (c) An inflated balloon
   (d) A woollen cloth

8. When hot air is passed through the coke, the following reaction takes place.

$$\text{Coke} \xrightarrow{\text{Hot air}} \underset{\text{Non-poisonous}}{A} + \underset{\text{Poisonous}}{B}$$

   Increased concentration of A is a cause of
   I. acid rain
   II. global warming
   III. greenhouse effect
   The correct answer(s) is/are
   (a) I and II   (b) II and III
   (c) Only II   (d) I, II and III

9. Ravi sort out some plastics into following two groups:

Group A

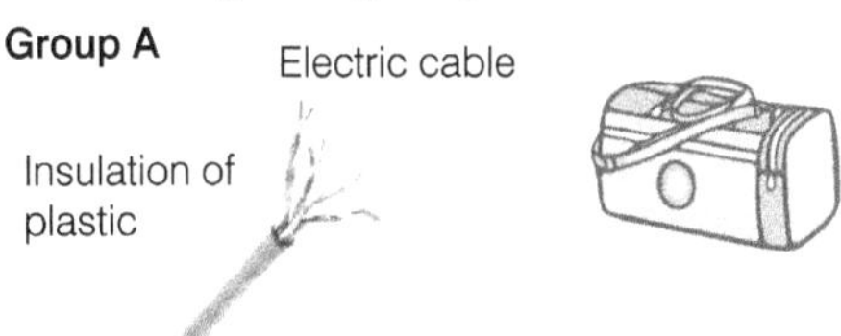

Group B

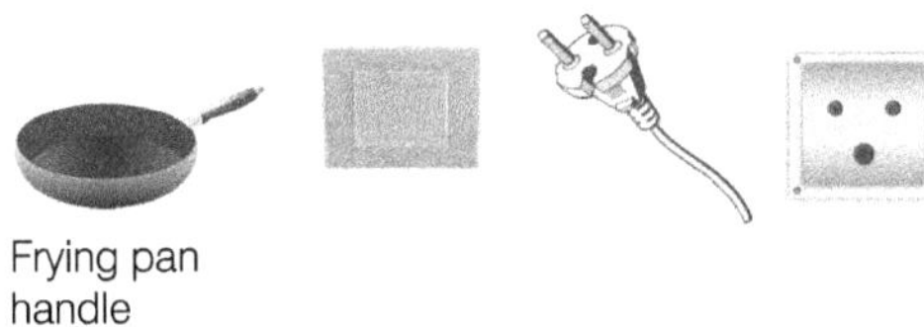
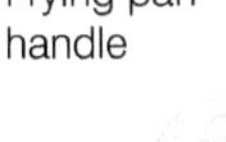

Which of the following shows a point of similarity and a point of difference between the above two groups?

	Point of similarity	Point of difference
(a)	Force of attraction	Mouldability
(b)	Force of attraction	Structure
(c)	Non-biodegradability	Conductivity
(d)	Inertness	Force of attraction

10. **Statement I** When sodium metal reacts with oxygen and water, a lot of heat is generated.

   Statement II Sodium metal is kept under kerosene.

   Which of the following statement(s) is/are correct?
   (a) Only I   (b) Both I and II
   (c) Only III   (d) None of these

11. Consider the following statements.
   I. Among all the naturally occurring elements, around 80% are metals.
   II. Non-metals are more abundant than metals.
   III. Sodium and potassium are soft like wax.
   IV. Bromine is a reddish brown solid at room temperature.

   The correct statements are
   (a) I, II and III   (b) II, III and IV
   (c) I, III and IV   (d) I and III

12. The focus is also called the hypocentre of an earthquake. The vibrating waves travel away from the focus of the earthquake in all directions. Directly above the focus on the Earth's surface is the earthquake's epicentre. Earthquake waves do not originate at epicentre.

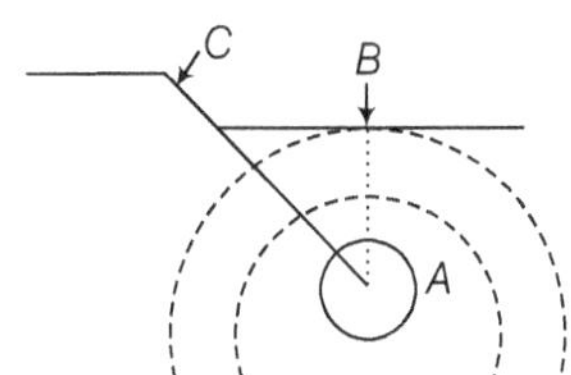

Point A where slip initiated during the earthquake is called the ....

(a) dip   (b) epicentre
(c) focus   (d) scarp

13. What force acting on parachute keeps it afloat for a few seconds before falling to the ground?
(a) Magnetic force
(b) Frictional force
(c) Gravitational force
(d) Both (b) and (c)

14. When several molecules of X are combined with several molecules of Y, a product is obtained, structure of which is given below.

$$-OH_2CH_2C-$$

$$O-\overset{\overset{O}{\|}}{C}-C_6H_5-\overset{\overset{O}{\|}}{C}-O-CH_2CH_2O-$$

$$\underbrace{\qquad\qquad\qquad\qquad\qquad}_{Z}$$

The unit Z here represents a
(a) polymer   (b) monomer
(c) repeating unit   (d) None of these

15. What may result when the environment becomes unfavourable to the organisms?
I. The organisms may die.
II. The organisms may adapt.
III. The organisms may move to another place.
(a) I and II   (b) II and III
(c) I and III   (d) I, II and III

16. **StatementI** Combustion of most fuels releases carbon dioxide in the environment.

Statement II Global warming is said to occur because of the decreased concentration of carbon dioxide in air.

Which of the following statement(s) is/are correct?

(a) Only I   (b) Only II
(c) Both I and II   (d) None of these

17. Metamorphosis is a reproduction process that involves transformation, opt the option that correctly defines the metamorphosis in butterfly.
(a) Pupa $\rightarrow$ Adult
(b) Larva $\rightarrow$ Adult
(c) Egg $\rightarrow$ Adult
(d) Adult butterfly emerging from pupa and egg

18. Match the following columns.

	Column I		Column II
A.	Friction produces	1.	Ceiling fan
B.	Wheels	2.	More friction
C.	Ball bearing	3.	Heat
D.	Rough surface	4.	Rolling friction

Codes

	A	B	C	D
(a)	4	3	1	2
(b)	3	4	2	1
(c)	3	4	1	2
(d)	4	1	2	3

19. Forces are invisible but they can be ....
A. felt   B. heard
C. seen in action   D. measured
(a) A and B
(b) A and C
(c) A, C and D
(d) A, B, C and D

20. Which of the following organisms are protected in Rann of Kutch Wildlife Sanctuary?
A. Wild ass   B. Flamingo
C. Desert fox   D. Asiatic lion
(a) B and C   (b) A and D
(c) A, B and C   (d) A, B, C and D

21. Which of the following does not lead to water pollution?
(a) Rainwater flows into the drain.
(b) Water from the sink flows straight into the sewer.
(c) Wastes from the chemical factories flow straight into the sea.
(d) All of the above

22. Which one of the following human activities has a negative impact on the environment?
(a) Recycling
(b) Reforestation
(c) Usage of chlorofluorocarbon (CFC) products
(d) Developing energy-efficient technology

23. Match the following columns.

	Column I		Column II
A.	Non-metal	1.	Jewellery
B.	Gold	2.	Wrapping food
C.	Aluminium	3.	Good conductor of electricity
D.	Copper	4.	Oxygen
		5.	Semi-conductor

Codes

	A	B	C	D			A	B	C	D
(a)	5	2	1	3		(b)	1	5	2	4
(c)	4	1	3	2		(d)	4	1	2	3

24. Lightning may appears in .... cycle.
(a) nitrogen
(b) water
(c) carbon
(d) electrical

25. Since, ancient time, X has been used for the large scale production of alcoholic drinks such as wine. The conversion of sugar to alcohol is known as Y.
Identify the process Y.
(a) Decantation
(b) Fermentation
(c) Decomposition
(d) Distillation

26. **Statement I** Formation of coal, petroleum and natural gas required a very high temperature and pressure.

Statement II Coal, petroleum and natural gas can be prepared in the laboratory.

Which of the following statement(s) is/are correct?
(a) Only 1
(b) Only II
(c) Both I and II
(d) None of these

27. A spring balance was used to measure the force needed to pull a wooden block across different surfaces. The table shows the results. The force is expressed in Newton. In which of the following is the friction greatest?

Floor surface	Force needed to just start moving
Carpet	10 N
Polished tiles	2 N
Polished wood	5 N
Thick rug	12 N

(a) Carpet
(b) Polished tiles
(c) Polished wood
(d) Thick rug

28. Air is a mixture of various gases. One of the gases is 21% part of the air and is essential for the survival of human beings. This gas is ....
(a) nitrogen
(b) oxygen
(c) ozone
(d) argon

29. A manufacturer has the following specification for outdoor tops.

Underline the name of the best fabric from the list given below.
(a) Cotton denim
(b) Wool twill weave fabric
(c) Cotton corduroy
(d) Polyester

30. When a glass rod is rubbed with a piece of silk cloth, the rod
(a) and the cloth both acquire positive charge
(b) becomes positively charged while the cloth has a negative charge
(c) and the cloth both acquire negative charge
(d) becomes negatively charged while the cloth has a positive charge

31. Match the following columns.

	Column I		Column II
A.	PVC	1.	Poor conductor of heat
B.	Melamine	2.	Polyester
C.	PET	3.	Thermoplastic
D.	Synthetics	4.	Melt on heating

Codes

	A	B	C	D
(a)	2	1	3	4
(b)	3	2	1	4
(c)	4	3	1	2
(d)	3	1	2	4

32. A pendulum oscillates 50 times in 5s. Find its time period.
(a) 10 s   (b) $\dfrac{1}{10}$ s   (c) 20 s   (d) $\dfrac{1}{20}$ s

33. **Statement** (I) Venus is the brightest planet in our solar system.

Statement (II) Venus reflects 70% of sunlight incident on it.

Which of the following statement(s) is/are correct?
(a) Only 1
(b) Only II
(c) Both I and II
(d) None of the above

34. Rahul was observing colour of flames produced by different sources.

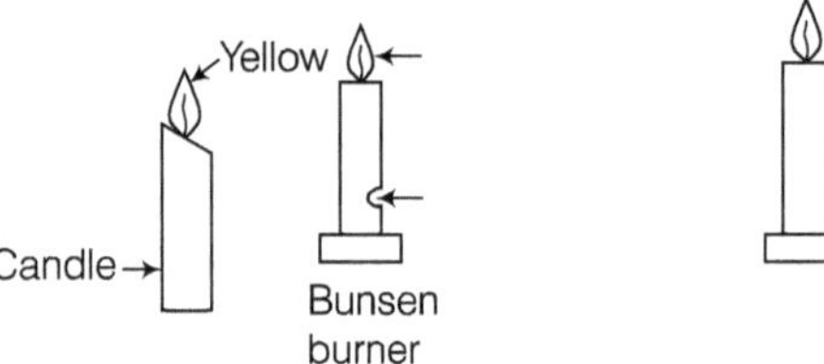

On the basis of his observations, he concluded that the colour of the flame depends upon
 I. the substance burning in the flame.
 II. the amount of oxygen available for combustion.
III. quantity of source used.
IV. temperature of the flame.

The correct observations are
(a) I, II and III
(b) I and II
(c) II and III
(d) I, II and IV

35. The teacher asked the children to make a statement about friction. Which of the student spoke correctly?

Alan Friction holds a nail in a wall.
Ayush Ball bearing help to increase friction.
Kavita We can reduce friction.
Anjana Life would be easy without friction.

(a) Alan and Ayush
(b) Alan and Kavita
(c) Ayush and Kavita
(d) Anjana and Ayush

36. Arrange the statements in sequence to show how global warming occurs and its effect.
    A. Carbon dioxide and harmful gases are released into the atmosphere.
    B. Temperature on the Earth increases.
    C. Fossil fuels are burnt.
    D. These gases trap the Sun's heat and prevent it from escaping into space.
    E. Ice at the poles melts.
    (a) A, D, C, B, E
    (b) B, D, C, A, E
    (c) C, A, D, B, E
    (d) B, E, A, C, D

37. We need friction for walking. To put a foot forward, we push the other foot backwards on the ground. The friction between our shoe and the ground acts in the opposite direction and prevents our foot from slipping. Thus, we are able to move forward.

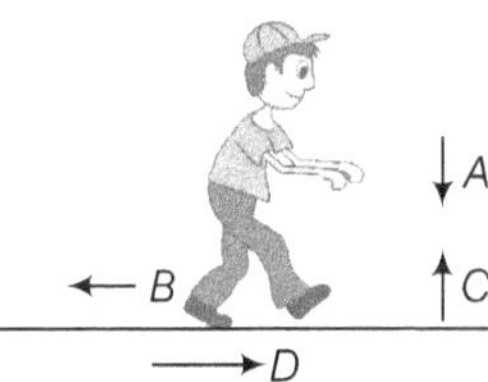

    In the above diagram, which arrow represents friction acting between the shoe and the ground?
    (a) A   (b) B   (c) C   (d) D

38. Food preservation ensures that the food lasts for a longer time without getting spoiled. Which of the following methods is used to preserve the food materials?
    (a) Drying and dehydration
    (b) Sterilization
    (c) Saltation and sweetening
    (d) All of the above

39. The animals found in a particular area are termed as fauna of that area. Consider the given animals and select that how many of these are examples of fauna of Pachmarhi Biosphere Reserve.

A.   B. 

C.  D. 

    (a) Only A
    (b) Only D
    (c) A and D
    (d) A, B, C and D

40. **Statement I** The chemical substances produced by microorganisms which in low concentration are antagonistic to the growth of other microorganisms are called as antibiotics.

    Statement II A preparation of a dead or attenuated pathogen, which when injected into a healthy person, provides immunity against a number of diseases, is called as vaccine.

    Which of the following statement(s) is/are correct?
    (a) Only I
    (b) Only II
    (c) Both I and II
    (d) None of the above

2 Marks Questions

41. Lightning can be seen, the moment it occurs. Aditi observes lightning in her area. She hears the sound 5 s after she observed lightning. How far is she from the place, where lightning occurs?

[speed of sound $= 330$ m/s]

(a) 1000 m   (b) 1550 m
(c) 1650 m   (d) 1750 m

42. Refer to the given Venn diagram and choose the correct option for P, Q and R.

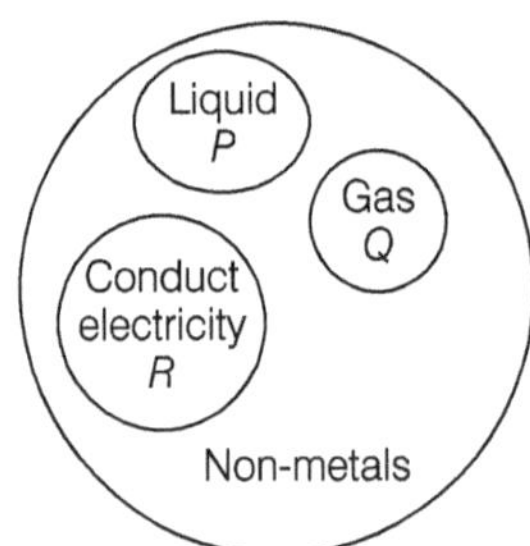

	P	Q	R
(a)	Mercury	Sulphur	Carbon
(b)	Bromine	Oxygen	Hydrogen
(c)	Mercury	Iodine	Oxygen
(d)	Bromine	Oxygen	Graphite

43.

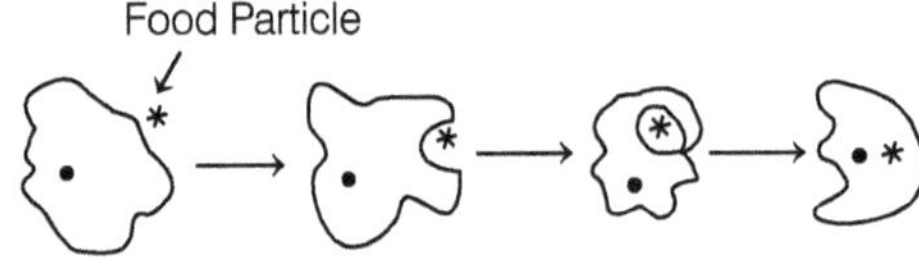

The above diagram shows
(a) Endomosis   (b) Phagocytosis
(c) Pinocytosis   (d) Exocytosis

44. Sohan made the following experimental set up and performed the same experiment by using three different threads, say, x, y and z.

His observation suggested him that the weights required to break the thread are in the order of $p > q > r$.

Here, $p =$ weight required in case of x

$q =$ weight required in case of y
$r =$ weight required in case of z

The threads x, y and z respectively are of
(a) nylon, wool and cotton
(b) nylon cotton and wool
(c) wool, cotton and nylon
(d) cotton, nylon and wool

45. A person goes through the stages of growth given below. Choose the correct sequence from the codes below.

1. Foetus   2. Zygote   3. Embryo
4. Baby   5. Adult
6. Adolescent 7. Child

Codes
(a) 2, 3, 1, 4, 7, 6, 5   (b) 2, 1, 3, 4, 7, 5, 6
(c) 3, 2, 1, 4, 6, 7, 5   (d) 1, 3, 2, 4, 7, 6, 5

46. Ram and Vaibhav performed experiments taking similar bulbs and cells but two different solutions A and B shown below.

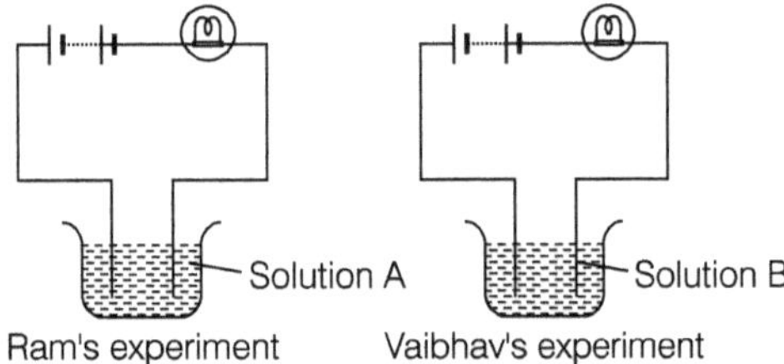

They found that the bulb in the setup A glows more brightly as compared to that of the setup B. You would conclude that
(a) Higher current is flowing through the circuit in setup A.
(b) Higher current is flowing through the circuit in setup B.
(c) Equal current is flowing through both the circuits.
(d) The current flowing through the circuits in the two setups cannot be compared in this manner.

47. Three friends, Salman, Adnan and Farhan argue as follows

Salman CNG is the least polluting fuel for vehicles.

Adnan Lignite is used for surfacing of road.

Farhan Petrol and diesel are the cleanest fuel for vehicles.

Who made the correct statement?
(a) Salman
(b) Adnan
(c) Farhan
(d) Adnan and salman

48. Which of the following statements describes the given microbe correctly?

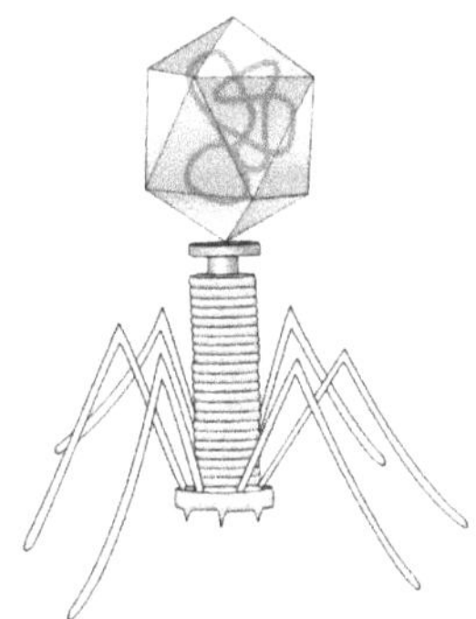

(a) It is a bacterium which causes diseases in plants
(b) It is a type of virus which attacks bacteria.
(c) It is a bacterium which kills viruses.
(d) It can multiply inside both living and non-living cells.

49. The pressure on the tyres of a sedan car is 220 kPa. The contact surface of each tyre with the floor is 200 cm^2. Calculate the new contact surface of each tyre when air is released from the tyre and the pressure of the car is reduced to 180 kPa.
(a) 240 cm^2
(b) 200 cm^2
(c) 245 cm^2
(d) 500 cm^2

50. Identify the incorrect labeling in the given diagram.

A $\rightarrow$ Eye spot

B $\rightarrow$ Nucleus

C $\rightarrow$ Chloroplast

D $\rightarrow$ Flagellum

E $\rightarrow$ Contractile vacuole

F $\rightarrow$ Pyrenoid

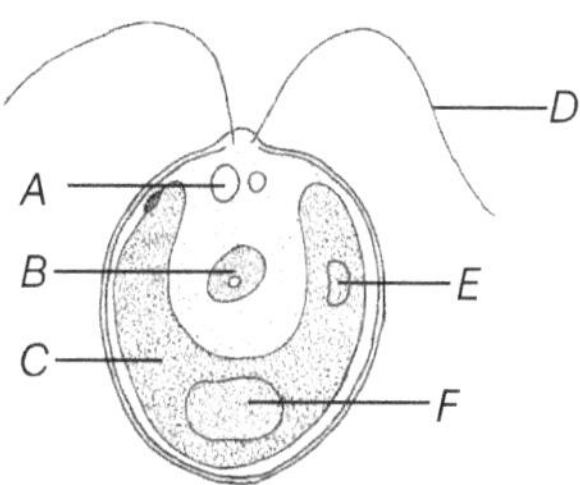

(a) Both A and E
(b) Both C and F
(c) Only D
(d) Only B

Hints & Solutions

Crop Production and Management

1. (*c*) Bean is a legume, not a cereal crop.

2. (*a*) Chemical fertilisers are rich in mineral acids which can increase the acidity in soil.

3. (*b*) In drip system, water falls drop by drop directly near the roots. In this method, water is not wasted at all, thus it is advantageous for areas facing water scarcity.

4. (*c*) Hoe is a simple tool which is used for removal of weeds and also loosening the soil.

5. (*a*) The soil is broken down into size of grain to loosen it for mixing nutrients, increase aeration, etc. Plough, hoe and cultivator are used for this process.

6. (*a*) Fungus (*Phytophthora infestans*) causes the blight of potato disease.

7. (*a*) Rice and soybean are Kharif crops which are sown at the onset of monsoon (July-October). This is because they require good water quantity and depend on rainfall patterns for their growth.

8. (*b*)

9. (*b*) To replenish the nutrients, farmers can add manures, left field uncultivated between two crops or perform crop rotation, i.e. leguminous crops between cereal crops. Excessive use of fertilisers can lead to soil acidification.

10. (*a*) Both the statements I and II are correct. Fertilisers are chemical substances supplied to crops to increase their productivity. They contain the essential nutrients required by the plants, including nitrogen, potassium and phosphorus. Urea, ammonium sulphate and superphosphate are some examples of fertilisers.

11. (*b*)

12. (*a*) Option (a) is incorrect. This is a traditional method of irrigation called as Dhekli used to draw water from wells, lakes, canals, etc.

13. (*c*) The correct identification of labels is
    P—legumes or pulses.
    Q—wheat, rice, barley, etc.
    R—sugarcane or beetroots.
    S—mustard, sunflower, groundnuts, etc.

14. (*c*)

15. (*b*) In sprinkler system, the water is allowed to pass through a system of pipes at a high pressure. This allows the nozzles to rotate and sprinkle water covering a large circular area. There is no deposition of water on ground thus, water logging is prevented.

16. (*d*)

17. (*a*) Beans, grams, peas, etc. are leguminous plants. These plants are capable of replenishing the depleted nitrogen levels in soil. These plants have *Rhizobium* living symbiotically within their roots, which is capable of fixing atmospheric N_2 and convert it into simple forms.

Microorganisms : Friend & Foe

1. (*c*) *Rhizobium* is a non-motile, rod-shaped bacteria, while others are of varying shapes and are motile.

2. (*a*) A bacterial cell is enclosed by a cell wall, with cytoplasm and a circular DNA which represents its nuclear material.

3. (*d*) Lichens are symbiotic association between a fungi (which provides shelter) and an algae (which manufactures) food with the help of photosynthesis). It is a mutually beneficial relationship.

4. (*d*) Chlorophyllous refers to the organisms containing chlorophyll, who can perform photosynthesis, e.g. *Chlamydomonas* as shown by figure (D).

5. (*c*) *Entamoeba* is a single-celled microbe, identified as a habitat of water bodies like lakes, ponds and rivers. It is found as internal parasite or commensals in the human gastrointestinal tract. They falls under the phylum-Protozoa.

6. (*b*) The organisms is bread mould, a type of fungus. It reproduces by spores, and is known to spoil the food materials. It absorbs nutrients from host's organism as well as from dead and decaying organism therefore have both mode of nutrition-saprophytic and parasitic.

7. (*a*)

8. (*c*) The statements II and IV are incorrect and can be corrected as, Bacterial cells lack a defined nucleus.
    Exchanging genetic information is not a method of sexual reproduction.

9. (*b*) *Spirogyra* can be used as a source of food. It consists of proteins, lipids, carbohydrates, dietary fibres, etc.

10. (*c*) In group C, all diseases are the caused by bacterial pathogens, i.e.
Anthrax—*Bacillus anthracis*
Typhoid—*Salmonella typhi*
Tuberculosis—*Mycobacterium tuberculosis*
Cholera—*Vibrio cholerae*

11. (*b*) Organisms like *Nostoc, Rhizobium* and *Anabaena* (helps in nitrogen fixation), *Lactobacillus* (curd formation), *Aspergillus* (secretes penicillin) are identified as beneficial for humans. While *Entamoeba* and *Bacillus anthracis* are pathogens.

12. (*b*) An antibiotic is a chemical substance secreted by a bacteria/fungi or other microbes which can kill or prevent the growth of disease causing bacteria.

13. (*b*) The incorrect statements II and III are can be corrected as
Foot and mouth disease of cattle is caused by a virus.
The bacterium which promotes the formation of curd is *Lactobacillus*.

14. (*c*) Statements III and IV are false and can be corrected as
- Yeast produces CO_2, not CH_4.
- Citrus canker is a bacterial disease transmitted through air.

15. (*b*) The process of conversion of atmospheric N_2 to simple easily usable forms (nitrates) for plants is called as nitrogen-fixation.

16. (*a*) *Rhizobium* lives in a symbiotic relationship with roots of leguminous plants, where it forms root nodules in which nitrogen-fixation takes place.

17. (*c*) Nitrogen present in atmosphere cannot be used by plants as such. Thus, conversion of atmospheric N_2 is carried out by different sources such as nitrogen-fixing bacteria, fungi and *Rhizobium* present in soil. Apart of them, lightening also help in the process of nitrogen fixation.

18. (*c*) Milk contains various types of bacteria which are harmless normally but at higher temperature they multiply rapidly and convert the lactose present in milk into lactic acid. This increases the acidity of milk, causing floting of protein and separation of liquid.

19. (*b*)

20. (*b*) The correct events are as follows,
At P—*Rhizobium* is forming root nodules where nitrogen-fixation occurs.
At Q—Nitrogen from air is being fixed.
At R and S—Nitrification occurs.
At T—Denitrification is taking place.

Synthetic Fibres and Plastics

1. (*b*) Silk is a natural animal fibre which is obtained from silkmoth. Whereas, nylon, lycra and polyester are synthetic fibres.

2. (*b*) Polyester being a synthetic fibre will melt when comes in touch with hot iron, so it should not be ironed.

3. (*c*) Nylon was the first fully synthetic fibre. It was made without using any natural raw material. It was prepared from coal, water and air.

4. (*c*) Cotton as well as paper are obtained from plants, so on burning, similar types of smell is obtained.

5. (*d*) Acrylic and nylon are synthetic fibres, i.e. obtained from artificial sources whereas cellulose is a natural fibre as obtained from natural sources. Rayon although is obtained from natural sources but by chemical modification, so it is called semi-synthetic fibre.

6. (*b*) Nylon is used for making parachutes and ropes for rock climbing. Nylon is also used for making socks, ropes, tents, toothbrushes.

7. (*a*) Polycot is a mixture of polyester and cotton and polywool is a mixture of polyester and wool. Cotton and wool are natural fibres.

8. (*d*) Synthetic fibres melt on heating and get stick to the body of the person wearing them. Further, they catch fire readily. That's why, clothes made up of these fibres should not be worn while bursting crackers.

9. (*b*) Synthetic fibres are generally light weight and fast drying and the fibres obtained from fish scales (except mermaids) show these properties.

10. (*c*) Because of its does not absorb water, more strength (even in wet condition) and resistance towards bacteria and fungus, nylon is used in making bristles of toothbrush.

11. (*d*) Polywool is made up of polyester and wool whereas polycot is made up of polyester and cotton. They have combined properties of each fibre and are made by blending synthetic (polyester) with natural (wool and cotton) fibres. They are less expensive also.

12. (*b*) Thermoplastics are those plastics, which gets deformed easily on heating and can be bent easily.

13. (*c*) Bakelite is an insulating material, so it absorbs electric shock for saving us and also prevent possible fire in electrical insulations. That's why, it is used in making electric plugs, switches, etc.

14. (*b*) Teflon is a special plastic on which oil and water do not stick.

15. (*c*) Facts I, II and III show that plastics are bad conductors of heat and electricity, whereas nylon is used to make parachutes.

16. (*d*) Polyvinyl chloride (PVC) can be coated on cloth to give a waterproof coating and is tougher than polythene so used in raincoats and seat covers.

17. (*d*) Plastics are non-reactive, light in weight, and durable. Plastics are bad conductor of electricity, that's why bakelite is used for making electrical switches. Bakelite is the example of thermosetting plastic.

18. (*d*) A material for making food container must be corrosion resistant, moulded into various shapes, can resist high temperature and should not conduct heat.

19. (*a*) Polyester is a non-wrinkable fabric. Rayon, because of its silk like appearance is used for the synthesis of cheap silk like clothes. Nylon, because of its strength is used for making parachute and stockings and flax is used in shrouds of Egyptian pharaohs.

20. (*d*) II (wool) and III (cotton) are natural fibres, so burn to form a residue.
I (nylon) and V (polyester) are synthetic fibres, so they melt on burning.
II (wool) and IV (silk) have proteins just like hair, so give smell of it on burning.

21. (*d*) Wool absorbs more water than silk and acrylic is a substitute for wool (not terylene). Strength of nylon is much higher as compared to cotton.

22. (*c*) Both P and Q are polymers. However, P is a linear polymer, but Q is a cross-linked polymer. The small circles in both the structures show the monomer units.

23. (*c*)

Metals and Non-metals

1. (*d*) Sonority is the property of metal to produce ringing sound. Tensile strength is the maximum load that a material can withstand by the longitudinal pull. The property of metal to be beaten into sheets is called as malleability whereas to be drawn into wire is called as ductility.

2. (*b*) Silver is a good conductor of heat as well as electricity.

3. (*a*) Pots and pans are made up of metals as hard, malleable and possess high melting point. The good electricity conducting property of metals is considered when these are used for making wires.

4. (*c*) The bulb will glow only in case of conductors. Out of the given materials, aluminium foil, iron nail and graphite are conductors but coal is a non-conductor.

5. (*b*)

6. (*b*) Corrosion is the process of deterioration (eating away) of metal from its surface when comes in contact of environmental factors like air, water, etc.

7. (*c*) Metals like nickel and chromium are highly resistant towards corrosion, so these are generally electroplated (coated over iron by the use of electricity) to protect iron from corrosion (or rusting).

8. (*a*) Copper turns green due to its corrosion. In this process, its surface gets covered by a layer of basic copper carbonate, i.e. it contains copper hydroxide and copper carbonate.

$$2Cu + H_2O + CO_2 + O_2$$

(Copper) (Water) (Carbon dioxide) (Oxygen)

Moist air

$$\longrightarrow Cu(OH)_2 + CuCO_3$$

(Copper hydroxide) (Copper carbonate)

Green coating

9. (*b*) Only highly reactive metals like magnesium, aluminium, etc. displace hydrogen from dilute acids, which burns with 'pop' sound.

$$Mg + 2HCl \longrightarrow MgCl_2 + H_2 \uparrow$$
$$2Al + 6HCl \longrightarrow 2AlCl_3 + 3H_2 \uparrow$$

10. (*d*) Sodium is so soft that it can be cut with a knife. Phosphorus reacts with air but not with water, so it is stored under water as it rapidly catches fire on coming in contact with air. Copper turns green when comes in contact of environmental factors (moist air).
Carbon on burning gives carbon dioxide, which is an acidic gas.

11. (*d*) A highly reactive metal displaces the less reactive metal from its salt solution. The order of reactivity of given metals is
$Ca > Mg > Zn > Fe > Cu$
Thus, reactions I and III are feasible.

12. (*b*) Iron being more reactive than copper, displaces copper from copper sulphate solution, so blue colour of copper sulphate fades.
$$\underset{\text{(Iron nail)}}{Fe(s)} + \underset{\text{(Copper sulphate)}}{CuSO_4(aq)} \longrightarrow \underset{\text{(Iron sulphate)}}{FeSO_4(aq)} + \underset{\text{(Copper)}}{Cu(s)}$$
Copper is less reactive than iron, so it cannot displace iron from its salt. Hence, no reaction takes place.

13. (*d*) Mercury does not stick with the glass and is easily visible. Further, it possesses a high boiling point and expands on heating. That is why, it is used in making thermometers.

14. (*c*) Brass is an alloy of copper and zinc. Bronze is an alloy of copper and tin. Steel is a homogeneous mixture of iron and carbon. Solder is a mixture of tin and lead.

15. (*b*) Since, the element contains 5 electrons in outermost shell, so to complete 8 electrons, it acquires 3 electrons, hence it is a non-metal. Further, it may be nitrogen, which is an inert element and filled in chips packets.

16. (*a*) Aluminium is used in making drink cans, foils (because of its inert nature) and aeroplanes parts (because of its lighter nature).

17. (*d*) P = Metal,　　Q = Non-metal
　　　R = Graphite,　S = Mercury

18. (*c*) Glass jar does not react with the acid present in pickle, so it is preferred for storing the pickle and prevent the pickle from spoiling.

19. (*b*) Turning of calcium hydroxide solution milky suggests that the oxide is of carbon or sulphur and both these elements are non-metals.
Hence, X is a non-metal.

20. (*a*) Since, X can displace Y from its salt solution, so X is more reactive than Y but less reactive than hydrogen.
Z and A both release hydrogen with dilute acids, so both are more reactive than hydrogen. Z releases hydrogen with nitric acid, so it may be Mg or Mn.
Further, A does not displace Z from its salt solution, so Z is more reactive.

Thus, the order of reactivity is
$$Z > A > X > Y$$

21. (*d*) All the given points are correct.
Reaction of metal and non-metal with oxygen
$$\underset{\text{(Metal)}}{4Na} + O_2 \longrightarrow \underset{\text{(Basic oxide)}}{2Na_2O}$$
$$\underset{\text{(Non-metal)}}{C} + O_2 \longrightarrow \underset{\text{(Acidic oxide)}}{CO_2}$$
Reaction with salt of less reactive element
$$\underset{\text{(Zinc)}}{Zn} + FeSO_4 \longrightarrow ZnSO_4 + \underset{\text{(Iron)}}{Fe}$$
Reaction with water
$$\underset{\text{(Metal)}}{2Na} + 2H_2O \longrightarrow 2NaOH + H_2\uparrow$$
$$\underset{\text{(Non-metal)}}{I_2} + H_2O \longrightarrow \text{No reaction}$$
Reaction with dilute acids
$$\underset{\text{(Metal)}}{2Na} + \underset{\text{(dil.)}}{2HCl} \longrightarrow 2NaCl + H_2\uparrow$$
$$I_2 + HCl \longrightarrow \text{No reaction}$$

22. (*c*) Metals and non-metals both form oxide on reacting with oxygen. The metallic oxides are generally basic while non-metallic oxides are acidic in nature.

Coal and Petroleum

1. (*d*) Coke and charcoal are amorphous allotropes of carbon whereas graphite is its crystalline allotrope. Thus, all these are its free form. Petrol is a mixture of several hydrocarbons (i.e. compounds of carbon and hydrogen).

2. (*c*) Exhaustible natural resources are limited in nature. They can be exhausted by human activities and are dependent on nature.

3. (*b*) Coke being a good reducing agent is usually used in the extraction of metals. Coal tar is used for synthesising plastics, paints, etc. Coal gas is a good fuel while coal is the remains of vegetation.

4. (*a*) Carbon dioxide, heat and water are formed as product after complete combustion of methane.

5. (*d*) All the given actions help in saving petrol.

6. (*a*) Bitumen is obtained from petroleum. Wildlife is an example of exhaustible natural resource. Bitumen is used for surfacing roads. Carbonisation is a very slow process.

7. (*c*) The given properties match with the coal tar so, this substance should be coal tar.

8. (*c*) Coke, coal gas and coal tar are the products of processing of coal while CNG is obtained from drilling for petroleum.

9. (*b*) The given statement indicates that X is the coal gas and from it water gas, producer gas and diamond can be prepared.

10. (*a*) Carbonisation is a very slow process of conversion of dead vegetation into coal. Since, coal is obtained from remains of vegetation, it is also called fossil fuel. A very high temperature and pressure is required for the occurrence of this process.

11. (*b*) Coal tar is used as a starting material for the synthesis of various items like synthetic dyes, drugs, explosives, perfumes, plastics, naphthalene balls (used to repel moths and insects), etc.

12. (*a*) Lignite is also known by the name brown coal and contains about 70% carbon.
    Anthracite is the purest variety of carbon as it contains about 90% carbon.
    Peat is the most impure form and contains only 60% carbon,
    Bituminous is the most common variety and is associated with 78% carbon.

13. (*b*) Coal tar is a mixture of ≈ 200 substances. Coke is the most pure form of carbon. It is a porous black material. Coal is a fossil fuel obtained by carbonisation process and it is used in thermal power plants for generating electricity.

14. (*a*) Energy from water and geothermal energy can be good alternative of coal in power station.

15. (*c*) Coal is made up of carbon along with small amounts of oxygen, sulphur, hydrogen and nitrogen. Its main varieties are peat, lignite, bituminous and anthracite. Among these, anthracite is the hardest and contains 90-95% carbon. Peat is the softest variety.

16. (*b*) X = Above, Y = Lighter

17. (*d*) Natural gas can be easily transported through pipes, so can be used as a fuel at homes for cooking. It can also be used for power generation. It is stored under high pressure as compressed natural gas (CNG), which is a good fuel for vehicles.

18. (*a*) Diesel. paraffin, CNG. bitumen and kerosene are the constituents of petroleum but coal tar and coal gas are obtained from coal.

19. (*c*) LPG-Liquefied Petroleum Gas (or petroleum gas in liquefied form). Natural gas can be converted into CNG (compressed natural gas)

by applying pressure. Petroleum is also known by the name black gold and paraffin wax is used in making vaseline, candles, ointments, etc.

20. (*c*) The order of different fractions from top to bottom is

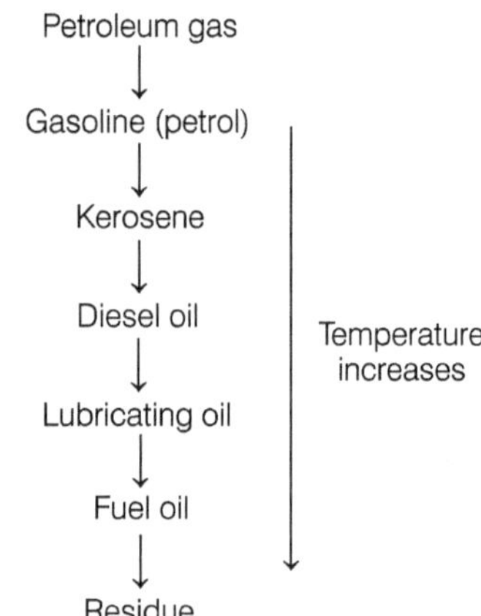

21. (*a*) Natural gas supplied to homes and factories through pipes and is obtained from oil wells. Natural gas is a cleaner fuel and exhaustible source of energy like fossil fuels.

22. (*b*) Boiling points of different hydrocarbons are different. Petrochemicals are obtained from petroleum and natural gas and are used in the manufacture of detergents, fibres, etc. Paraffin wax is used of making candles, vaseline, polish, etc.

23. (*b*) Kerosene (paraffin oil) lies in between the petrol and diesel oil. This fraction is used as a fuel for stoves, lamps and jet engines.

24. (*a*) X = coal, Y = limited, Z = always

25. (*c*) Coal is obtained by carbonisation process which is a very slow process (i.e. takes thousands of years) and requires very high temperature and pressure. Existence of such conditions in laboratory is not possible, so coal cannot be prepared in the laboratory.

26. (*b*) The petroleum is subjected to fractional distillation to obtain products of various uses. All other statements are true.

27. (*c*) Fossil fuels should be conserved because they are available only in limited quantity. Resources present in limited quantity are called exhaustible resources.
    Burning of coal in insufficient amount of oxygen produces carbon monoxide, not carbon dioxide.

Combustion and Flame

1. (*b*) The necessary conditions for combustion are availability of air/oxygen, fuel and temperature of fuel is more than its ignition temperature.

2. (*d*) Combustion reactions are those reactions which take place slowly and given less amount of heat slowly is called slow combustion. i.e. burning of candle, burning of wood, burning of paper.

3. (*d*) In this experiment, it is seen that candle is burn in glass chimney in which sufficient oxygen is present. So, this experiment shows that, oxygen is essential for combustion.

4. (*c*) Ignition temperature of sulphur is high enough, so it does not burn in air at room temperature.
   During spontaneous combustion, the material suddenly bursts into flame.
   All other given statements are true.

5. (*c*) Carbon monoxide is a particles of unburnt carbon (X) added to the environment which leads to respiratory and nervous diseases (Y).

6. (*c*) Burning of candle is an example of slow combustion, burning of phosphorus is example of spontaneous reaction (combustion), burning of LPG is an example of rapid combustion and burning of crackers is an example of explosion.

7. (*a*)

8. (*d*) When hole is open, oxygen is in excess, so complete combustion takes place and the colour of the flame is blue. When the hole is close, oxygen supply is not sufficient for the complete combustion of the fuel. Due to incomplete combustion of the fuel, the colour of the flame is yellow.

9. (*d*) Energy is largest in non-luminous zone. Outermost zone is the hottest part of the flame. Some fuels burn with flame while some are not.

10. (*c*) Dark zone is the coldest zone, so it takes highest time as compared to two other zones to reach at 50°C.

11. (*a*) For a good fuel, ignition temperature should be low but calorific value should be high.

12. (*b*) Smoke causes respiratory problems, carbon monoxide chockes the throat, oxides of nitrogen causes lung diseases and dust causes allergic reaction.

13. (*c*) Total mass of fuel $= 4.5\,$kg
    Total heat produced $= 180000\,$kJ
    Heat produced by burning 1 kg of fuel
    $$= \frac{180000}{4.5}\,\text{kJ/kg}$$
    $$= 40000\,\text{kJ/kg}$$

14. (*c*) Increased concentration of carbon dioxide in the environment result in increased temperature of the Earth, which is known by the name global warming.

15. (*d*)

16. (*b*) Ignition temperature of A (hydrogen) is very low because of which it catches fire immediately and hence, cannot be considered as an ideal fuel.

17. (*a*)

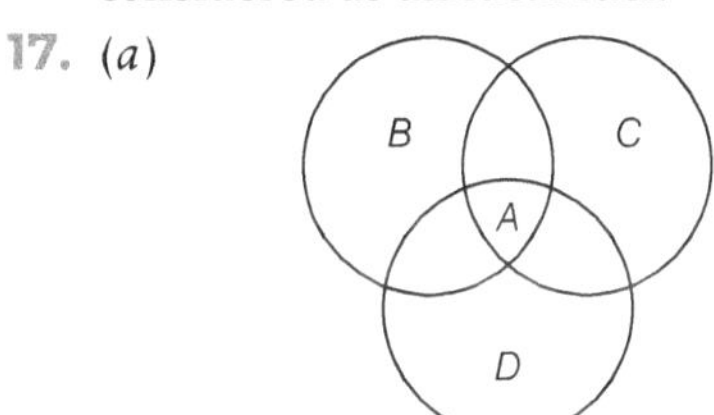

A—Natural fuels,	B—Wood
C—Coal,	D—Cowdung cake

18. (*c*) When fuel is burnt, oxides of sulphur and nitrogen are produced. These oxides when dissolve in rainwater, makes it acidic. Such rain is called acid rain.

19. (*b*) Magnesium is a combustible substance and combustion is a chemical process (not a physical process).
    All other given statements are true.

20. (*b*) In rapid combustion, material burns rapidly to give heat and light.
    During explosion, sound is also produced along with heat and light. Baking soda is a fire extinguisher as it produces CO_2 gas on burning.
    In case of spontaneous combustion, the material burns without any apparent cause.

21. (*b*) If change A is a chemical change, then, B must be a physical change which is reversible in nature.

Conservation of Plants and Animals

1. (*d*) The animals who are very few in numbers and thus on verge of being extinct are labelled as critically endangered in Red Data Book.

2. (*b*) Kaziranga National Park in Assam is protected area where conservation projects for one horned rhinoceros are under going.

3. (*b*) The tiger is not an extinct species because living members of this species are still present.

4. (*b*)

5. (*b*) This picture is of a flightless bird called Dodo, that was endemic to island of Mauritius. Since there is no living member of this species on Earth, hence it is now extinct.

6. (*b*) Deforestation impacts all parts of the Earth. It results in reduction of groundwater level, atmospheric moisture, rainfall pattern, etc. The level of CO_2 will rise along with other pollutants. This will lead to increased greenhouse effect and global warming.

7. (*c*) *P* is man made place called zoos, while *Q* is conservation of wild animals in their natural habitats, i.e. wildlife sanctuary.

8. (*a*) Endemic species are those species of plants and animals which are found exclusively in particular area. They often threatened due to introduction exotic species from some other geographical area.

9. (*b*) All the given strategies can be adapted to save our environment except IV. Keeping birds and animals in our house is not a feasible action.

10. (*c*) Deforestation is cutting down of forests for human requirements. This results in disturbed water cycle which affects rainfall, decrease in groundwater levels, increase in floods and droughts.

11. (*b*) Birds who fly distance to reach another land to avoid inhospitable weather conditions of their habitats are called migratory birds. Siberian crane fly for laying eggs as the weather is their natural habitat becomes very cold and inhospitable.

12. (*a*)

13. (*b*) Deforestation removes the trees which hold the soil together by their roots. Removing the trees leaves the soil bare to wind and other elements which lead to soil erosion due to lack of humus and fertility of soil. This ultimately lead to desertification.

14. (*d*) Dianosours became extinct due to large scale climatic change which eliminated most of the life from the Earth. Food chain imbalances lead to the starvation of the dinosaurs.

Cell : Structures and Functions

1. (*b*) Red blood cells are enucleated cells. These cells flow as part of blood throughout the body. Their main function is to deliver oxygen to the body tissues.

2. (*b*) *Euglena, Chlorella* and *Chlamydomonas* are unicellular, i.e. single celled organisms.

3. (*c*) The cell is identified as a neuron which works with brain, spinal cord and our body parts and helps in transmission of neural impulses in our body.

4. (*b*) Humans are multicellular eukaryotes is made up of different types of cell. Yeast is single-celled eukaryotic organism. *E.coli* is classified as a prokaryote, having one cell and no well-defined nucleus.

5. (*a*) The organisation of body starts from simplest structure, i.e. cell → cluster of cells called tissues → organ → organ system and organism (the most complex form).

6. (*c*) Cell was discovered by Robert Hooke. Rest other options are correct.

7. (*a*) The shape and size of a cell is related to its function and not depends upon the body size of the organism.

8. (*c*) Rose, ginger and lotus are plants with many cells, i.e. they are multicellular, while yeast, *Amoeba* and *Paramecium* are unicellular, i.e. they are single-celled organisms.

9. (*d*) Part *A* is the outer cell wall present in plant cells additional to cell membrane. It protects the plants from environmental variations and injury causes by animals.

10. (*a*) Cell membrane is a biological membrane that is semipermeable in nature. It facilitates transport of substance across the cell. But the membrane of dead cell loses this ability of transporting substances therefore allows all substance to enter into the cell.

11. (*c*) Part labelled *B* is the nucleus which acts like the control centre monitoring all the activities been carried out within the cell.

12. (*d*) In animal cells, mitochondria is the kitchen where energy is produced, while in plant cells, it is the chloroplast where photosynthesis takes place.

13. (*a*) In plant cell, cell wall (*A*), chloroplast (*B*) and a large central vacuole (*G*) is present which are not found in animals.

14. (*b*) Among the four mentioned structures, cell wall and chloroplasts are not found in animal cells, whereas cell membrane and cytoplasm are present in animal cells.

15. (*b*) The organelle *X* is mitochondria. Its folded projections in inner membrane are called cristae *Y*.

16. (*c*) Leaf is a part of plant and blood is from humans or animals. Both these cells have nucleus and mitochondria which represents the *X*. Whereas animal cell lacks cell wall and chloroplast.

17. (*a*)

18. (*b*) As the organism can be seen by naked eyes which means it is not a unicellular organism. Also the organism is an animal which are multicellular in nature.

19. (*d*) Robert Hooke, in 1665 discovered cell by observing a piece of cork under his microscope. Schleiden defined the cell as the basic unit of plant in 1838, and a year later, Schwann defined the cell as the basic unit of animal structure.

20. (*a*) *A*- is the cilia which helps in movement of mucus and bacteria.
B- is the nucleus which controls activities of cells.
C is the cell membrane which regulates the movement of substance across the cell.
D- is cytoplasm in which cell organelles are suspended.

21. (*c*) *X* is endoplasmic reticulum where lipids are synthesised in cell, while *Y* is the vacuole that make a plant cell turgid and maintains water balance.

22. (*b*) The correct match descriptions are
A. If cell wall is absent, cell will loses its regular shape.
B. A cell will have no control over its activities if nucleus is missing from the cell.
C. In absence of cell membrane, the cell will not be able to filter what passes in and out of cell.
D. In absence of chloroplast, cell will not be able to do photosynthesis and make food.

Reproduction in Animals

1. (*d*) *B* is the uterus where a fertilised egg undergoes development to form a baby.

2. (*d*) Mature sperm travel through vas deferens from testes and then forwarded to urethra after adding secretion from semniferous tubules and passes into penis.

3. (*a*) A male foetus is formed when *X* and *Y* chromosomes pair up from mother and father, respectively while a foetus is female when *X* and *X* chromosomes pair up from mother and father, respectively

4. (*a*) Animal *X* is starfish. This method is called as external fertilisation where fusion of gametes take place outside of a female body.

5. (*c*) *X*–Ova, *Y*–Sperm and *Z*-Zygote. Ova is a female reproductive cell which fuse with the male reproductive cell-sperm to form zygote.

6. (*a*)

7. (*a*) Only statement (a) is true. The correct form of other statements are
- Young ones do not necessarily look the same to parents who undergo metamorphosis.
- Life cycle of silkworm involves → egg → caterpillar → pupa → adult.
- A tadpole lives in water as they have gills whereas frog can live on land and in water because lungs replace the gills.

8. (*b*) The organisms is *Hydra* in which asexual reproduction occurs through budding.

9. (*c*) In figure *A*, binary fission in *Amoeba* and in *B*, budding in yeast is depicted. Both these are the methods of asexual reproduction.

10. (*c*) At stage *D*, cytokinesis, i.e. the division of cytoplasm equally among daughter cells takes place.

11. (*b*) Regeneration is the ability of some organisms to form new individuals from their body parts, e.g *Planaria* and starfish show regeneration. Whereas *Amoeba* does not regenerate.

12. (*a*) Both A and R are true, and R is the correct explanation of A. Cloning helps in preserving parental features because the genetic material from parents is copied and propagated asexually.

13. (*c*) In the animals who exhibit viviparity, i.e. which produce young ones, the process of fertilisation, growth and development of embryo to foetus occurs inside female parent's body.

14. (*d*) Statements I, II and IV are incorrect. The correct form of these statements are
- Human females are viviparous as they give birth to young ones.
- An egg is fertilised by only one sperm.
- After 9 months of development in mother's uterus, the baby gets ready for delivery.

15. (*b*) Statements II and IV are incorrect. The correct form of these statements are
- The animals that lay eggs are known as oviparous animals.
- Snakes exhibits internal fertilisation, i.e. fusion of gametes take place inside the animal's body.

16. (*c*) Statements I and III are false. The correct form of these statements are
- Fertilisation is not a necessary event is asexual reproduction
- Clones are produced by asexual reproduction.

Age of Adolescence

1. (*c*) The larynx grows larger in size during the puberty. It protrudes out at the front of the throat especially in boys.

2. (*b*) Oestrogen is the female hormone whose production starts when girls reach puberty. It is secreted by ovary and is responsible for appearance of secondary sexual characters in females.

3. (*c*) The appearance of hair in the armpits and pubic area is a common changes at puberty in both the male and female sexes.

4. (*a*) Puberty begin at the age of 12-14 years in males and at 10-13 years in female. This phase is of rapid growth and development.

5. (*d*) The first menstrual period is called menarche. It marks the beginning of a woman's reproductive cycle. Menopause is a natural biological process in which the menstrual cycle stops. It marks the end of a woman's reproductive cycle.

6. (*b*)

7. (*a*) Adolescents grow at a faster rate and thus require proper, healthy diet. This diet gives sufficient nutrients, which are used in growth of the body.

8. (*c*) The insulin hormone is known to lower the blood sugar level. Thus, the doctor has prescribed insulin injection to this patient because he has high blood sugar level.

9. (*d*) Iodine is essential for proper functioning of thyroid gland.

10. (*d*) Trypsin is the odd one out because it is an enzyme, while others are hormones.

11. (*c*) Adrenaline hormone prepares the body for a fight or flight response. In preparation for it, our heartbeat, breathing rate, blood pressure and glucose metabolism increases. Thus, option (c) is correct.

12. (*b*) I depicts the effect of adrenaline secreted from adrenal glands (*G*), while II represents the effects of insulin secreted from pancreas (*H*).

13. (*c*) The figure is showing the condition called goitre. It develops due to deficiency of thyroxine hormone (which requires iodine for its production). Due to this, the thyroid gland enlarges and neck swells too much.

14. (*a*) Gland *X* is the pituitary which secretes the growth hormone. The secretion of less hormone results in dwarfism in which body does not grow and person remains very short while excess hormone results in gigantism, i.e. body grows extremely tall.

15. (*a*) *X* represents the process of fertilisation, i.e. the fusion of male and female gametes. If it happens then the zygote divides to form embryo which gets implanted in uterine wall and establish pregnancy. In absence of fertilisation, the uterine line is shed as menstrual bleeding.

16. (*a*) Endocrine glands secrete hormones directly into the bloodstream from where they reach the target site, e.g. pituitary, adrenal and thymus gland.
Exocrine gland secretes substances onto an epithelial surface using a duct, e.g.—sweat, salivary, prostate gland, etc. Liver and pancreas have both exocrine and endocrine functions.

17. (*a*) Part labelled *P-S* are correctly identified as
- *P*—Ovary, site of gamete production.
- *Q*—Fallopian tube, site of fertilisation.
- *R*—Uterus, site of development of embryo.
- *S*—Vagina, passage for entry of sperms.

Force and Pressure

1. (*d*) A force is a push or a pull which can change the state of rest or motion of an object. It can change direction of motion. A force can also change the speed of a moving object.

2. (*d*) Friction opposes the state of an object. The force needed to push the box is least for *D*. Therefore, friction will also be least for *D*.

3. (*b*) Attractive magnetic force acts between the electromagnets and the metallic hammer which makes the hammer strike the gong.

4. (*d*) The deep treads on the tyre are to increase friction. As rough surface has more friction. Thus, it reduces the chance of slipping.

5. (*b*) Gravitational force and magnetic force extend the spring, whereas elastic force tries to move the spring back.

6. (*c*) Friction is a force and unit of force is newton (N).
Weight $= mg =$ Force.
This implies that weight is also a force.
So, unit of weight is also in newton (N).

7. (*d*) When the girl tries to walk, she pushes the ground backward due to which the ground provides a frictional force to the feet in the forward direction, i.e. in the direction of walking (*D*).

8. (*b*) The spring *B* is compressed most as compared to the other springs due to the greater weight of woman at this point of chair.

9. (*c*) The effect of the force depends on the magnitude of force and the area of surface on which it is applied. The effect of force takes place in the direction of the force applied.

10. (*d*) The object does not fall as the tension in the string acts against the weight or Earth's gravity.

11. (*b*) Match II and III are correct, but I and IV are incorrect. In case I, the button on the top of pen is pushed while in case IV, the object placed on the book is pulled upward.

12. (*c*) As, pressure is given by, $p = F / A$ Thus, increasing area of contact reduces the pressure on their heads.

13. (*d*) The lorry least likely to sink is the one which exerts the smallest pressure on the soft ground.
Since, pressure $= \dfrac{\text{force}}{\text{area}}$
So, the lorry least likely to sink has the smallest weight and the largest number of wheels, i.e. an empty lorry with six wheels.

14. (*a*) As, *B* and *C* have same vertical depth. Thus, pressure on both the points (which is equal to height × density of water) will be same and thus, water will flow out at same pressure from these taps.

15. (*a*) The pressure will be maximum for position *A* as area of contact is least in Fig. (*A*) and pressure = force/area.

16. (*c*) Water exerts pressure in all directions at any given depth.
Therefore, it exerts pressure on the wall as on the bottom of the bucket.
Hence, both statements are correct.

17. (*b*) The air molecules inside a balloon collides and create a large pressure on the boundary of balloon, thus increasing its size.

18. (*d*) The pressure exerted by a liquid depends on the vertical depth of the liquid. From the diagram, the water level in each container has the same vertical height. So, the pressure exerted will be same in each vessel.

19. (*d*) Pressure increases with the increase in depth. Thus, pressure at $A<$ pressure at $B<$ pressure at C.

20. (*c*) Pressure, $p = \dfrac{\text{force}}{\text{area}}$
Here, force = weight = 80 N
and area = area of contact with ground
$$= 10 \times 5 \, \text{cm}^2$$
$$\therefore \qquad p = \dfrac{80}{10 \times 5} \, \text{N/cm}^2$$

21. (*c*) When pressure is applied on closed liquid in a container, then it is transmitted equally in all the directions inside it.

22. (*c*) As the paper clip move along the ramp, frictional force work between the ramp and the clip, magnetic force attracts the paper clip and gravitational force is trying to keep the paper clip down.

23. (*a*) Friction is acting in all the three cases. In cases I and II, air friction acts on objects while in case III, the frictional force due to brakes slow down the bicycle.

24. (*a*) A running child applies force with the help of his muscles and this makes him run faster. The air molecules applies force (force = pressure × area) on the walls of the balloons which inflates the balloon.
A woman applies force by her muscles and moves a stationary object. A cricketer applies the force in the opposite direction of the movement of ball and stops it.

25. (*b*) The force of gravity is same for all tubes as they are identical and have same amount of toothpaste initially.
As more amount of toothpaste is accumulated on plate below tube 1 than that below tube 3, so more force is applied on tube 1 and more amount of toothpaste is left in tube 3.

26. (*b*) Pressure is the force applied on a unit area of contact and is given by, $p = F / A$
Its SI unit is pascal or Pa.
Hence, only statement *B* is incorrect.

Friction

1. (*c*) When the box is moved across the floor, frictional force comes into play. It acts in opposite direction to the motion of the box and makes the box to stop.

2. (*a*) The direction of friction is always opposite the direction of motion. Force *D* is the action force that the shoe exerts on the ground. The reaction force, i.e. the friction acting on the shoe opposes the force *D* and hence acts in the direction of *A*.

3. (*b*) The direction of friction *F* always opposes the direction of the pulling force *P*.
The weight of object '*w*' always acts vertically downwards from the centre of gravity of the object.

4. (*c*) The road applies a friction force whenever a car is moving or at rest. When brakes are applied the friction of the road will help the car to stop. The greater the friction the lesser time it will require to stop the car. Hence, the smaller distance will be covered.

5. (*c*) She is least likely to slip on bricks as it will provide maximum friction to her due to its rough surface.

6. (*d*) The force of friction acts between two surfaces irrespective of whether the object is solid, liquid or gaseous.

7. (*b*) Friction acts in opposite direction to the motion of object. Moreover, it acts between the surfaces. Thus, the force of friction in the given case will act on the box from left to right ($\rightarrow$).

8. (*a*) Friction will be maximum at *P* as it is most rough.

9. (*c*) Friction always opposes the applied force. So, the force must be applied in the direction of *R*.

10. (*a*) As the roughness of surface increases the friction increases. Hence, the correct order of increasing force of friction is
wet marble floor < dry marble floor < newspaper < towel.

11. (*c*) Frictional force is the opposing force acting in case of ball moving. This cause, the ball to stop after a while.

12. (*a*) Maximum distance is covered on the surface having least friction. Among given surfaces, icy surface has least friction. So, stone cover maximum distance on icy surface.

13. (*b*) Lubricating hinge of door with oil decreases friction and hence, movement of door becomes smooth.

14. (*c*) To reduce friction, boy should spread talcum on the wooden surface. A thin layer is formed over the surfaces in contact and they do not directly rub against each other. Interlocking of irregularities is avoided to a great extent and hence, movement becomes smooth.

15. (*c*) Sliding friction is smaller than static friction. Rolling fricting is still smaller than the sliding friction.
Hence, the correct order is
Static friction > sliding friction > rolling friction.

16. (*a*) Static friction is greater than sliding friction. It is more difficult to bring a body into motion from the rest than to keep a body moving.

17. (*b*) Rocket, bird, etc., have streamlined shape to reduce the area of contact with air and hence to reduce air friction.

18. (*c*) Frictional force acts in opposite direction to that of the motion, i.e. in direction *S*.

19. (*a*) Rollers reduce the friction in roller-skates.

20. (*b*) Friction can be reduced by using rollers, lubricants, ball bearing, etc.

21. (*a*) As the object is at rest, so static friction acts on it. Static friction always becomes equal to the applied force until body starts moving. Hence, when the applied force is doubled, then friction is also doubled.

22. (*c*) Lubricants, streamlined bodies, polished surface and ball bearing reduce friction. However, heat does not reduce friction. But friction can produce heat.

23. (*d*) Friction is more on a dry floor than a wet floor.

24. (*d*) As rolling friction is much less than that of static friction between two surfaces in contact, so its value must be less than 20 N.

25. (*b*) Friction acts on an object opposite to the direction of its motion irrespective of whether it is moving or not.

26. (*b*) Without friction we can't live happily because all the objects are moving due to friction.

Also, if we move by any kind of external force, then we can't stop ourselves, if friction is not present in nature. So, the life will not be easy.

27. (*c*) Friction occurs because most surfaces are not smooth. Friction opposes motion.

28. (*c*) I. The force of friction is independent of the area of the surfaces in contact.
    II. Friction opposes motion.
    IV. Solids and liquids do not allow things to move over in them, without any external force.

29. (*d*)

30. (*a*) Rough surfaces provide more friction. Wheels decreases the area of contact between the tyre and surface and hence, reduces the friction. Submarines and rockets have streamlined bodies to reduce air friction. In space or vacuum, there is no friction.

Sound

1. (*c*) In a whistle, the air column vibrates to produce sound.

2. (*c*) This type of instrument is called jal tarang.

3. (*c*) Sound waves are material waves, i.e. they need a medium for their propagation. Sound waves cannot travel in vacuum.
   So, sound could not be heard in given case.

4. (*b*) Sound needs a medium to propagate. So, it will travel in all given media except vacuum.

5. (*c*) More the air-column, more is the vibration. Hence, the intensity of sound will be maximum in the jar filled less than half.

6. (*d*) Sound waves require a medium in order to be transmitted. In a glass jar with no air, there is a vacuum which cannot transmit sound.
   Similarly, in outer space, there is also a vacuum which cannot transmit sound.

7. (*b*) Speed of sound is fastest in a solid, slower in a liquid and slowest in a gas.
   So, given order is air < water < steel.

8. (*a*) As sound travels faster in solids. So, the person is able to hear an approaching train.

9. (*c*) Except tabla and piano, all are string based instruments.

10. (*c*) Sound requires a material medium for its propagation, while light does not.

11. (*d*) Eustachian tube does not vibrate itself. It carries the sensation of vibration of sound from inner ear to brain.

12. (*b*) The tartar is removed by a scalar, having a hook at its one end.

13. (*a*) Range of audible human sound frequency is 20 Hz (or 0.02 kHz) to 20000 Hz (or 20 kHz). Hence, 100 kHz is above the normal audible range.

14. (*b*) The middle part of the ear amplifies the sound and it consists of three bones hammer, anvil and stirrup.

15. (*a*) Sound waves with frequencies less than 20 Hz are called infrasonic waves.

16. (*c*) The frequencies determine the pitch of a sound and the amplitude determine the loudness.
    Noise is the irregular vibration, while music is the regular vibration.

17. (*c*) Total time = 20 s, speed = 1.5 km s^{-1}
    $\therefore$ Depth of the sea, $d = \dfrac{\text{speed} \times \text{total time}}{2}$
    $$= \dfrac{1.5 \times 20}{2} = 15 \text{ km}$$

18. (*b*) The pitch of a sound depends directly on the frequency. Higher the frequency higher will be the pitch. Thus, sound produced by bees which are not carrying honey has a higher pitch.

19. (*c*) Higher the frequency, higher the pitch and higher the shrillness of sound and *vice-versa*.
    So, IV and V are odd.

20. (*b*) Distance = speed × time
    $= 330 \times 5 = 1650 \text{ m} = 1.65 \text{ km}$

21. (*d*) Given, $f = 500$ vibrations/s $= 500$ Hz
    Time-period, $T = \dfrac{1}{500} = 0.002$ s

22. (*a*) The loudness and pitch of sound depends on amplitude and frequency of the sound wave, respectively. So, for louder note of higher pitch, the amplitude and frequency will be larger than the first.

23. (*d*) II. Sound requires a medium to travel but light can travel in vacuum.
    III. Sound propagates in all directions.

24. (*b*) II. Sound higher than 20000 Hz is called ultrasonic.
    IV. Ultrasonic waves are used to measure the depth of a sea.

25. (*b*) II. Sudden exposure to high noise can cause a hearing impairment.
    III. Use of amplifiers and loudspeakers should be restricted.

26. (*d*) I. Ultrasonic waves are used to kill bacteria in liquids.
II. Infrasonic waves are produced by the vibration of the Earth's surface during the Earthquake.

27. (*a*)

Chemical Effects of Electric Current

1. (*d*) Sodium ions are positively charged, so they are attracted towards negative electrode. Similar is the case with chlorine ions.

2. (*b*) Milk, honey and glass are bad conductors of electricity, whereas water with impurities is a good conductor of electricity and pure water is bad conductor.

3. (*c*) Saline water is a good conductor of electricity. So, scientist must add salt to it.

4. (*a*) An electrochemical cell, the electrode connected to positive terminal of a battery is called anode and that connected to the negative terminal is called cathode.

5. (*b*) Conduction tester is used determine whether a substance is a good or poor conductor of electricity.

6. (*c*) Non-metals are poor conductors of electricity as they do not have conduction electrons.

7. (*d*) An electric current can produce chemical, heating and magnetic effects.

8. (*a*) The change in colour of the solution is due to the chemical effect of current.

9. (*d*) An electrolyte should be able to dissociate into ions (positive and negative) so that the ions can move and lead to current.

10. (*d*) Distilled water is a bad conductor of electricity. Sugar solution also does not conduct electricity very well.

11. (*c*) As, the ends of metallic wire are not connected to the battery, so the circuit is not closed and no current flows in the circuit. Then, electrons move in random directions, so that the resultant effect will be zero.

12. (*b*) Metallic ions are positive ions which get deposited on cathode.

13. (*d*) Sodium chloride, copper sulphate and silver nitrate are good electrolytes whereas sugar solution is a bad conductor of electricity.

14. (*d*) Seawater is very salty and salt solution is a good conductor of electricity. Larger current produced by seawater produces greater magnetic field thus more deflection.

15. (*a*) The water used by fireman to douse fire is ordinary water that contains minerals and impurities. So, it is a good conductor of electricity. Hence, to prevent electrocution, they shut off electricity supply.

16. (*d*) The flow of electric current through a conducting solution causes chemical reaction due to which any or all of the mentioned changes can take place.

17. (*a*) LED's consumes much lower electricity. So, they are economical. Also, they are available in many colours. LED has applications in many purposes. Ordinary bulb can glow only when the current supply is sufficient to give its wattage value.

18. (*c*) Silver, gold and chromium are used for electroplating.

19. (*d*) Conduction tester is used to find the conductivity of material whether it is good or bad conductor. Iron fillings do not form continuous conducting path, so they can't be used in conduction tester.

20. (*d*) In the electroplating factories, the disposal of the used conducting solution is a major concern. It is a polluting waste and there are specific disposal guidelines to protect the environment.

21. (*b*) CFL has a very small amount of mercury (about 4g) sealed inside. LED are much cheaper and cost efficient than CFL. An electric circuit is a closed conducting path in which an electric current flows. Milk is a bad conductor of electricity.

22. (*b*) II. All wires used in electric circuits should be covered with non-conducting material.
III. Heating effect of the current is responsible for the glow of bulb in an electric circuit.
V. Anode is positive electrode.

23. (*c*) The correct match is
Insulator $\rightarrow$ Distilled water
Conductor $\rightarrow$ Sea water
Electrolyte in lemon juice $\rightarrow$ Citric acid
Non-metal $\rightarrow$ Poor conductor

24. (*d*)

25. (*d*) Rain water is a conductor of electricity because of presence of ions. Metals are more conducting than the electrolyte. It is because solid metals have excess electrons on surface and hence better conductor than liquid.

Some Natural Phenomenon

1. (*b*) A lightning conductor is a device used to protect buildings from the damaging effects of the lightning. If lightning strikes the building, the lightning conductor provides an easy path for the lightning bolt to pass through the ground.

2. (*a*) When storm clouds are developed during thunderstorm, strong wind move upwards and the clouds rub against each other. Due to this friction charges are developed in the clouds. The upper layers of clouds get positively changed and the lower layers get negatively charged.

3. (*c*)

4. (*d*) The top of the cloud becomes positively charged while the base of the cloud becomes positively charged. Thus, both charges are stored in clouds.

5. (*b*) The pointed end of umbrella may attract lightning, so an umbrella should be avoided during lightning and thunder.

6. (*d*) If one is travelling by a car during lightning, he is safe inside the car with windows and doors of car shut. Because metallic body of a car prevents lighthing to hit a person inside. The lightning gets discharged to the ground by metallic frame of the car.

7. (*c*) Ozone gas is formed in air during lightning that absorbs ultraviolet radiation present in the sunlight.

8. (*a*) The clothes are rubbed against each other and thus static charge is developed between the clothes.

9. (*a*) It is because light travels much faster than sound. Speed of light is 3×10^8 ms^{-1} and speed of sound is 342 ms^{-1}.

10. (*a*) Mobile phones and cordless phones do not have a conducting path for lightning as landline phones have. This makes them safer to use during lightning or thunderstorm.

11. (*a*) Lightning conductor can protect buildings from the effect of lightning. One end of the lightning rod is kept out in the air and other is kept burried in the ground. Electrical lights must be unplugged during a thunderstorm.

12. (*d*) A seismograph is the instrument that is used to detect an earthquake. It consists of a seismometer, which may be a pendulum mounted on a spring.

13. (*d*) Lightning is just a strong electric discharge, so it cannot cause tsunami.

14. (*a*) The earthquake is caused by the disturbance deep down inside the uppermost layer of the earth called the crust.

15. (*a*) Earthquake is caused by the movement of plates. The boundaries of the plates are the weak zones where earthquakes are more likely to occur. The weak zones are also known as seismic or fault zones.

16. (*a*) The Earthquake can cause floods, landslides and tsunamis.

17. (*b*)

18. (*c*) Electrograph is not related to the Earthquake. It is used for tracing actions of electrical devices.

19. (*b*) Tsunamis are caused by earthquake, landslide or volcanic eruptions on the sea floor. An earthquake is caused by the movement of tectonic plates and thus this earthquake on the sea floor can cause tsunamis.

20. (*b*) I. Electroscope is a device which tests whether an object is carrying charge or not.
    II. A lightning conductor protects building from the effect of lightning by the process of earthing.
    IV. In an electrical storm, the upper portion of the cloud is positive and the lower portion is negative.

21. (*b*)

22. (*c*) If you live in the earthquake prone area, then
    I. You would keep an emergency kit always ready.
    II. You would have a closed book shelves and closed cupboards.
    III. You would fix the cupboards to the walls.
    IV. You would not keep breakable items on the upper shelves.

23. (*c*) For each whole number increase in magnitude, a ten fold increases in the intensity of Earthquake occurs. Thus, the tremors at *B* is 100 times those of place *A*.

Light

1. (*d*) When all the parallel rays reflected from a plane surface are not parallel, the reflection is known as diffused or irregular reflection. For Fig. (B), incident rays are parallel but the reflected pattern is not parallel.

2. (*c*) Light can be reflected from any point or part of the mirror.

3. (*b*) When all the parallel rays reflected from a plane surface are not parallel, then reflection is known as diffused or irregular reflection. It is caused by the irregularities in the reflecting surface.

4. (*a*) $\angle AOC + \angle i = 90°$

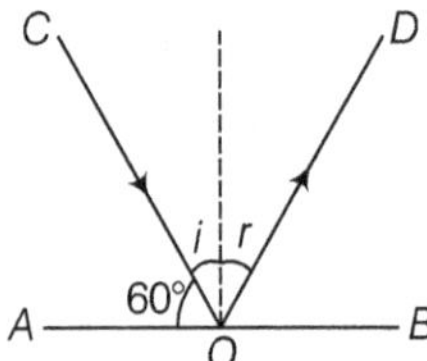

$$\Rightarrow \qquad \angle i = 90°-60° = 30°$$
$$\therefore \qquad \angle i = \angle r = 30°$$

5. (*d*) Infinite images are formed when two plane mirrors are placed parallel and facing towards each other with object between them.

6. (*c*) $\angle i + 40° = 90° \Rightarrow \angle i = \angle r = 50°$

7. (*d*) All the rays will follow the laws of reflection. Hence, angle of incidence will always be equal to the angle of reflection in all three cases.

8. (*c*) The image formed by a plane mirror is upright, virtual, of the same size as the object, and as far behind the mirror as the object is in front of it.

9. (*d*) Distance of test card from the plane mirror (behind the mirror) $=150\,cm$
Distance of man from the mirror $=100\,cm$
Thus, distance of man from the image of test card $=150 + 100 = 250\,cm$

10. (*a*) Due to lateral inversion in mirror time 8 : 50 will be seen as 3:10.

11. (*d*) Mirage is an optical illusion which is caused due to atmospheric refraction of light.

12. (*a*) As we move up from ground or surface of Earth, the atmospheric pressure decreases and so, the density of air decreases. This is the cause of optical illusion.

13. (*d*) The ciliary muscles contract and loosen to change the focal length of lens to focus the image of objects at varying distances.

14. (*c*) When we enter in a dark room our pupil expands to allow maximum light to pass through it and it takes some time.

15. (*b*) Rods are the rod-shaped cells of the retina that are sensitive to the dim light.
Cones are cone-shaped cells of the retina that are sensitive to the colours of light.

16. (*b*) Lens in our eyes is convex lens.

17. (*c*) Accommodation is the ability of the eye to change its focus from distant to near objects. It is achieved by changing the shape of eye lens.

18. (*c*) The focal length of the eye lens increases when eye muscles are relaxed and lens becomes thinner. In increasing the focal length the muscles become contracted and lens becomes thicker.

19. (*d*) The iris controls the adjustment of size of pupil for changing brightness of light. It is the coloured part of the eye.

20. (*d*) Rods sense the brightness of light. Cones functions in bright light and sense the colour of light.

21. (*c*) There is a slight difference between the images formed by left and right eye individually. Our brain combines both the images to give a three dimensional view.

22. (*c*) The retina of human eye has an ability to retain the image of an object for one-sixteenth of a second even after the removal of the object. This is called persistence of vision and used in moving picture applications like cinematography.

23. (*b*) Sun, stars, glowing tubelight and fire are luminous objects because they emit their own light.
Moon, Earth and table are non-luminous objects because they do not emit their own light.

24. (*a*)

25. (*b*) Diffused reflection is not due to the failure of the laws of reflection. It is caused by the irregularities in the reflecting surface.

26. (*d*)

27. (*b*) A person of 1m long in front of a plane mirror seems to be 1m from the image. Splitting of white light into its constituent colours is known as dispersion. According to the laws of reflection, $\angle i$ is equal to $\angle r$.

28. (*c*) The correct match of columns is
Cataract $\rightarrow$ cloudy eye lens
Cornea $\rightarrow$ front part of eye
Blind spot $\rightarrow$ junction of optic nerve and retina
Persistence of vision $\rightarrow$ 1/16th of a second

29. (*a*) The size of the pupil becomes large when you see in dim light. Night birds have less cones then rods in their eyes. Cinematography works on the principle of persistence of vision.

Stars and Solar System

1. (*b*) The heat and light of stars is produced by the nuclear fusion reaction taking place inside them.

2. (*d*) The coolest stars appear red, while the hottest stars are blue which is much hotter then Sun.

3. (*b*) Orion and Cassiopeia are the constellations, which are visible in night sky during winter season.

4. (*a*) The position of Pole Star remains constant w.r.t. the Earth which is above the North pole.

5. (*d*)

6. (*c*) A light is the measurement unit for astronomical objects. If a star is 10 light year away from Earth, it means light from that star has taken 10 years to reach Earth surface and that information is 10 years old.

7. (*d*) Only Q is correct. The corrected form of rest are,

	A	B
P.	Planets do not have their own light	Stars have their own light
R.	Planets orbit around the stars like Sun	Stars do not revolve around planets

8. (*a*) The change in the position of stars is due to the rotation of Earth on its axis.

9. (*a*) There is a large gap in between the orbits of Mars and Jupiter. This gap is occupied by a large number of small objects that revolve around the Sun. These are called asteroids.

10. (*b*) Among given planets Venus and Mercury have no Moon. Moons are the natural satellite around the planets.

11. (*c*) Planet saturn, comets and asteroids are members of solar system. Cassiopeia is a constellation which is not a part of solar system.

12. (*a*) More the acceleration due to gravity more will be the ability of planet to pull the things towards itself. So, on jupiter ball will fall the fastest.

13. (*d*) Seasons happen because Earth's axis is tilted with respect to the plane of its orbit. Hence, different parts of Earth receive more or less solar energy at different times of year.

14. (*a*) Moon is the natural satellite of Earth. It does not have its own light but reflects the Sun's light falling on it. So, we see only that part of the Moon which reflect light toward us.

15. (*c*) As the bright portion of both Moon and Earth is towards C. So, the Sun's light is falling from this side.

16. (*a*) The first day of a month is the new Moon day. The next day only a small portion of the Moon appears in the sky. The Moon grows larger and larger every day. On the fifteenth day, we get a full view of the Moon.

17. (*a*) Since, Venus rotates from East to West direction. Sun will appear to rise from West and set in East.

18. (*d*) Pluto was earlier counted as a planet but not anymore. It is now called a dwarf planet.

19. (*d*) X is Ursa Major constellation. The other name is Great Bear. Seven bright stars are usually observed in X.

20. (*c*) Orion is called the hunter. The saptarishi appears like a big tadle or a question mark.

21. (*d*) A meteor which reaches the Earth's atmosphere is called meteorite. A meteor is called shooting star.

22. (*d*) The tail is always directed away from the Sun. The length of the tail grows as it approaches the Sun.

23. (*a*) Here, $1 \text{ m} = \dfrac{1}{9.4 \times 10^{15}}$ ly

$$\frac{1 \text{ m}}{1 \text{ s}} = \frac{\dfrac{1}{9.4 \times 10^{15}}}{\dfrac{1}{86400}}$$

$$= 9191.49 \times 10^{-15} \text{ m}/\text{s}$$

$$3 \times 10^{8} \text{ m}/\text{s} = 9191.49 \times 10^{-15} \times 3 \times 10^{8}$$

$$= 2.75 \times 10^{-3} \text{ ly day}^{-1}$$

Pollution of Air and Water

1. (*d*) The insecticide will accumulate in highest concentration in the topmost organism of the food chain, i.e. the eagle.

2. (*b*) *Escherichia coli* is a coliform bacteria that is found in human intestine. If this bacteria is found in sample, then the water has been most likely polluted by sewage.

3. (*c*) CO_2 is a greenhouse gas which absorb the sunlight reflected back by Earth's surface. This heat warms the Earth's surface (Green house effect). Thus, temperature will be lesser than the present.

4. (*d*) A rise in temperature will cause most of the ice caps and glaciers to melt. As a result of which the water level in surrounding oceans, seas will rise.

5. (*c*) Frog and toads have thin porous skin which absorbs more pollutants in comparison to other amphibians. This make them more prone to harmful effects of pollutants.

6. (*b*) Minamata is a neurological disease caused by mecury poisoning. Blackfoot disease is caused by drinking arsenic polluted water. Cadmium and its compound are highly toxic. They cause liver and lung cancer. Cholera is a bacterial disease.

7. (*c*) *X* is radon. Radon has no colour, no taste or odour, is a radioactive noble gas and it contributes to air pollution.

8. (*d*) All the statements are correct.

9. (*d*) Construction work will contribute to all types of pollution in the environment. Use of heavy machines and tools cause noise pollution, dust and fine particulates materials will cause air pollution and washed off will contribute to water pollution.

10. (*b*)

11. (*b*) Dried leaves on burning will release smoke and other gases that causes air pollution.

12. (*b*) CNG, i.e. Compressed Natural Gas should be used in vehicles to reduce air pollution.

13. (*c*) Deforestation is cutting down of trees. Reforestation will help in maintaining the CO_2 levels in atmosphere and reducing the consumption of fossil fuels will help in controlling global warming.

14. (*b*)

15. (*a*) In the wastewater treatment the first step is flow equilisation and then aeration of polluted water, then all the impurities of water are removed and at last the disinfection is used to remove all the infectious bacteria or microbes.

16. (*a*) Trees are planted along the roadside to reduce pollution from motor vehicles. They reduce pollution by absorbing traffic noise, taking in carbon dioxide and trapping dust and root from the exhaust pipes of vehicle.

17. (*b*) BOD is the Biological Oxygen Demand, a measure of O_2 required by microbes for decomposing a unit mass of organic substances.

18. (*d*) Only statement II is false while others (I, III and IV) are correct. The correct form of false statement is as follows
Excess greenhouse gases traps large amount of heat which leads to warming of Earth's surface.

19. (*a*) Mary is reusing the water and reducing the use of clean water.

Practice Set 1

1. (*c*)	2. (*d*)	3. (*d*)	4. (*b*)	5. (*a*)
6. (*b*)	7. (*c*)	8. (*c*)	9. (*a*)	10. (*b*)
11. (*d*)	12. (*c*)	13. (*b*)	14. (*a*)	15. (*b*)
16. (*b*)	17. (*b*)	18. (*d*)	19. (*b*)	20. (*a*)
21. (*b*)	22. (*c*)	23. (*a*)	24. (*d*)	25. (*c*)
26. (*a*)	27. (*b*)	28. (*b*)	29. (*c*)	30. (*a*)
31. (*c*)	32. (*a*)	33. (*b*)	34. (*c*)	35. (*c*)
36. (*b*)	37. (*c*)	38. (*a*)	39. (*c*)	40. (*c*)
41. (*c*)	42. (*a*)	43. (*c*)	44. (*b*)	45. (*c*)
46. (*d*)	47. (*b*)	48. (*c*)	49. (*d*)	50. (*c*)

Practice Set 2

1. (*c*)	2. (*c*)	3. (*c*)	4. (*b*)	5. (*d*)
6. (*d*)	7. (*b*)	8. (*c*)	9. (*d*)	10. (*b*)
11. (*d*)	12. (*c*)	13. (*b*)	14. (*c*)	15. (*d*)
16. (*a*)	17. (*b*)	18. (*c*)	19. (*c*)	20. (*c*)
21. (*a*)	22. (*c*)	23. (*d*)	24. (*b*)	25. (*b*)
26. (*a*)	27. (*d*)	28. (*b*)	29. (*d*)	30. (*d*)
31. (*d*)	32. (*b*)	33. (*c*)	34. (*d*)	35. (*b*)
36. (*c*)	37. (*d*)	38. (*d*)	39. (*d*)	40. (*c*)
41. (*c*)	42. (*d*)	43. (*b*)	44. (*a*)	45. (*a*)
46. (*a*)	47. (*a*)	48. (*b*)	49. (*c*)	50. (*a*)